Tenors in a lyric tradition

Peter Anders
Walther Ludwig
Fritz Wunderlich

with valuable assistance from Clifford Elkin

Discographies compiled by John Hunt

CONTENTS

3   Acknowledgement

4   Introduction

7   Peter Anders discography

85   Walther Ludwig discography

173   Fritz Wunderlich discography

281   Credits

Tenors in a Lyric Tradition
Published by John Hunt.
© 1996 John Hunt
reprinted 2009
ISBN 9780952582-77-9

Cover illustration shows LP label for a Peter Anders Lieder recital published by Melodiya from Reichsrundfunk tapes

Published 1996 by John Hunt
Designed by Richard Chlupaty, London

Copyright 1996   John Hunt

Sole distributors:
Travis & Emery,
17 Cecil Court,
London, WC2N 4EZ,
United Kingdom.
(+44) 20 7 459 2129.
sales@travis-and-emery.com

ACKNOWLEDGEMENT

This publication has been made possible by contributions from the following sponsor subscribers

Richard Ames, New Barnet
Stathis Arfanis, Athens
Yoshihiro Asada, Osaka
Jack Atkinson, Tasmania
J.M. Blyth, Darlington
A. Brandmair, Munich
J. Camps-Ros, Barcelona
Edward Chibas, Caracas
F. De Vilder, Bussum
Richard Dennis, Greenhithe
John Derry, Newcastle-upon-Tyne
Erik Dervos, London
Hans-Peter Ebner, Milan
Shuntaro Enatsu, Miyakonojo City
Henry Fogel, Chicago
Peter Fulop, Toronto
Philip Goodman, London
Jean-Pierre Goossens, Luxembourg
Johann Gratz, Vienna
A. Greenburgh, New Barnet
Peter Hamann, Bochum
Michael Harris, London
Donald Hodgman, Riverside CT
Martin Holland, Sale
Richard Igler, Vienna
Bodo Igesz, New York
Eugene Kaskey, New York
Shiro Kawai, Tokyo
Detlef Kissmann, Solingen
Eric Kobe, Lucerne
John Larsen, Mariager
Ernst Lumpe, Soest
John Mallinson, Hurst Green
Carlo Marinelli, Rome
Finn Moeller Larsen, Virum
Philip Moores, Stafford
Bruce Morrison, Gillingham

W. Moyle, Ombersley
Alan Newcombe, Hamburg
Hugh Palmer, Chelmsford
Laurence Pateman, London
Tully Potter, Billericay
Yves Saillard, Mollie-Margot
Helger Steinhauff, Stemwede
Yoshihiro Suzuki, Tokyo
H.A. Van Dijk, Apeldoorn
Hiromitsu Wada, Chiba
Urs Weber, St Gallen
Nigel Wood, London
G. Wright, Romford

TENORS IN A LYRIC TRADITION

With the departure of Richard Tauber in the mid 1930s as a result of Germany's new racial policies, the position of leading lyric tenor was open to any number of aspirants. Two of the likeliest candidates were just beginning their careers, **Peter Anders** (1908-1954) having made his debut at Heidelberg in 1932 and **Walther Ludwig** (1902-1981) already having appeared at Glyndebourne in 1935.

Both of these singers were subsequently prevented by the intervening war years from fully realising their international reputations, yet their work for the leading German stages and radio and record organisations was documented for posterity in a methodical way which was typical of the period. High quality recording techniques following the war-time introduction of magnetic tape enable listeners to follow the progress of these men right up to the time when **Fritz Wunderlich** (1930-1966) was taking his first steps in the profession. In 1954 Anders died as the result of a tragic car accident, and around the same time Ludwig was preparing to retire and return to the medical profession for which he had originally studied before taking up singing.

It is tempting to read a tragic destiny into the fact that Wunderlich was to be granted less than a decade at the top of the profession before he too died through a cruel accident. 1949-1966 was indeed a sad period for the musical world, with the losses not only of Peter Anders and Fritz Wunderlich but also of Ginette Neveu, Dinu Lipatti, Dennis Brain, Kathleen Ferrier and Guido Cantelli!

Listening to these three tenors without any restraints of sound quality, one might suppose that they are more modern in their approach - direct, unsophisticated and without idiosyncrasy - than other tenors of the period (Patzak, Dermota and Pears come to mind). Some of that youthful directness springs itself from the lyric tenor repertory, the beautifully constructed and ingratiating roles of Nicolai, Lortzing, Smetana, Massenet and Donizetti which were the preserve of these voices. All three of them shone in the part of the ardent dreamer Lensky in Tchaikovsky's **Evgeny Onegin**, or Lyonel in

Flotow's **Martha**. We cannot predict if, for example, Wunderlich might have ventured into the role of Max in Weber's **Der Freischütz** or even into heavier territory (a special affinity for the uniquely German spirituality of Pfitzner's **Palestrina** is already evident in Wunderlich's live Viennese recording of that part); Peter Anders was, admittedly, already flexing his vocal chords in the directions of Florestan in Beethoven's **Fidelio,** not to mention Verdi's **Otello** or Stolzing in Wagner's **Meistersinger.** Yet this surely was a healthy and natural development. The pressure which nowadays exists for a singer to have a "direction" (dictated by commercial reasons) rather than just doing what comes naturally to the voice, was unknown to these lyric voices.

The world of **Operetta** and the lighter muse was a springboard for all three, Anders and Ludwig being lucky enough to work in an era when the 78rpm record was the ideal way to present such a repertoire. Again, one must feel nostalgia for the past and regret, too, that German and Viennese operetta has (with exceptions) lost much of its fascination for the music-loving public, the result being that aspiring young singers now have no chance to explore it. Just after the war in Germany, however, there was still a voracious appetite for operetta, and one realises that it was an area where the re-emerging record companies relied heavily on the German radio stations: most of the operetta material which Anders recorded for DG/Polydor was taken from tapes originally prepared by Cologne's West German Radio.

A wealth of **Lieder** recordings is preserved in these discographies, both senior men again being fortunate to have been involved, in war-time Berlin, in Michael Raucheisen's project to record the entire German Lied repertoire for the Reichsrundfunkgesellschaft. It will be noted that some of this material remains unpublished: certain items appear only on LPs produced by Russian Melodiya because it was the Russians who confiscated many Reichsrundfunk tapes after 1945, but much can hopefully still be unearthed both in East and West. On the subject of Lieder, it is interesting to note that neither Anders nor Ludwig essayed the major song cycles of Schubert until 1945 or after. Wunderlich remains a special case here, with commercially recorded Lied performances which do not meet the requirements of some connoisseurs. However, I would like to plea for a re-assessment, for the extra dimensions afforded in live Lieder recitals recorded in Salzburg, Hannover and Edinburgh - with many more interesting risks being taken than in the subdued studio editions - point to what might still have developed if time had not run out.

The discographies are arranged chronologically under composers and set out in three columns: first column gives place, month and year in which recording took place (particularly in the early LP era, recordings were often spread over a period of time within the month or year); second column gives other participating soloists, orchestra and conductor or accompanying pianist; third column contains catalogue issue numbers. I have aimed at giving the first issue, subsequent editions in the most important territories in the various formats (45,LP,CD). I do attempt, for artists of particular import in the USA, to include American catalogue numbers which I can trace, but am always glad to hear from US collectors who can add to my information. As already explained, selected unpublished tapes, mainly from radio transmissions, are included in the hope that they might still be traced and found worthy of publication.

A word about the opera **Querschnitte** or highlights which were particularly popular in Germany during the LP era, but which already existed in the days of 78s, when a disc would contain mere sections from arias or ensembles joined together either by the conductor or technicians to form a potpourri. The actual contents of the 78rpm disc was not necessarily indicated on the label. It should therefore be borne in mind, and this also applies to LP highlights, that alternative recordings of individual operatic arias by the same artist may exist within a Querschnitt or highlights compilation.

John Hunt 1996

Peter Anders
1908-1954

Discography compiled by John Hunt

ADOLPHE ADAM (1803-1856)

Le postillon de Lonjumeau, Excerpt (Mes amis, écoutez l'histoire!)

Berlin November 1935	Städtische Oper Orchestra Schultze Sung in German	78: Telefunken A 1901 LP: Telefunken HT 2/KT 11007
Cologne June 1937	Orchestra Kühn Sung in German	Unpublished radio broadcast

LUDWIG VAN BEETHOVEN (1770-1827)

Fidelio

Hamburg December 1948	Role of Florestan Wegner, Guilleaume, Pfeifle, Roth, A.Welitsch NDR Orchestra and Chorus Schmidt-Isserstedt	Unpublished radio broadcast Excerpts LP: Allegro 3066 LP: Gramophone (USA) 20130-20131 LP: Acanta DE 23.316-23.217/ BB 23.311/40.23528 CD: Acanta 43.268 DE 23.316-23.317 incorrectly dated 1952
Naples April 1951	Rest of cast not traced San Carlo Orchestra & Chorus Fricsay	Unpublished radio broadcast
Geneva November 1951	Werth, Otto, Weiser, Metternich, Frick, Pantscheff Suisse Romande Orchestra & Chorus Fricsay	Unpublished radio broadcast

10 Anders

Fidelio, Excerpt (Gott! Welch Dunkel hier!)

Berlin March 1952	Städtische Oper Orchestra Rother	78: Electrola DB 11543 LP: Electrola E 60006/E 83380/WCLP 781 LP: EMI 1C 147 29142-29143M CD: EMI CDM 769 6822
Baden-Baden April 1952	Südwestfunk Orchestra Ackermann	Unpublished radio broadcast

Fidelio, Excerpt (Mir ist so wunderbar)

Berlin June 1942	Fuchs, Eipperle, Hann Berlin RO Rother	45: DG EPL 30 532 LP: BASF 22 21491-7 CD: Acanta 43.268

Symphony No 9 "Choral"

Berlin   Briem, Höngen,   LP: Melodiya D 010851-010854/M10 10851 009
March 1942   Watzke   LP: Unicorn UNI 100-101
               Kittel Choir   LP: Nippon Columbia DXM 105-106
               BPO   LP: Turnabout TV 4346-4347/TV4353-4354
               Furtwängler   LP: French Furtwängler Society
                                       SWF 7003-7004
                                   LP: Everest SDBR 3241
                                   LP: EMI 3C 153 53810-53816M
                                   LP: Toshiba WF 60045-60046
                                   LP: Movieplay (Spain) 11.0090-11.0091
                                   CD: Palette PAL 1025
                                   CD: Priceless D 13256
                                   CD: French Furtwängler Society SWF 891
                                   CD: Music and Arts CD 653
                                   CD: Classical Disk 880.456
                                   CD: Hunt CDWFE 357
                                   CD: Toshiba CE28 5748-5749/TOCE 8521
                                   CD: Melodiya MEL 10 00715
                                   CD: Documents LV 919-920
                                   CD: Historical Performers (Japan) HP 6
                                   CD: Grammofono AB 78581
                                   CD: Tahra FURT 1004-1007
                                   CD: Dante LYS 071
                                   <u>Sound of final bars from this recording
                                   also added to a newsreel film fragment of
                                   another Furtwängler performance, in which
                                   tenor soloist is Helge Rosvaenge</u>

Adelaide (Einsam wandelt dein Freund)

Berlin June 1943	Raucheisen	LP: DG 88 018 LP: Acanta 40.23535 CD: Berlin Classics BC 21672

An die ferne Geliebte, Song cycle

Berlin June 1943	Raucheisen	Unpublished radio broadcast
Cologne October 1948	Weissenborn	Unpublished radio broadcast <u>Tapes destroyed</u>
Stuttgart April 1951	Giesen	LP: Telefunken HT 36/DP 648.064

Lied aus der Ferne (Als mir noch die Trauer)

Berlin June 1943	Raucheisen	LP: DG 88 018 LP: Acanta 40.23535 CD: Berlin Classics BC 21672

<u>Beethoven Lieder sung by Anders also appear on Eterna LPs 820 445/822 611</u>

GEORGES BIZET (1838-1875)

Djamileh

Berlin June 1935	<u>Role of Haroun</u> Kern, With Funkorchester and Chorus Rosbaud <u>Sung in German</u>	Unpublished radio broadcast

12 Anders

Carmen, Excerpt (La fleur que tu m'avais jetée)

Berlin November 1934	Städtische Oper Orchestra Schmidt-Isserstedt <u>Sung in German</u>	78: Telefunken E 1761 LP: Telefunken HT 2/KT 11007
Cologne June 1937	Orchestra Kühn <u>Sung in German</u>	Unpublished radio broadcast
Berlin September 1937	Reichssender Orchestra Steiner <u>Sung in German</u>	Unpublished radio broadcast
Baden-Baden April 1952	Südwestfunk Orchestra Ackermann <u>Sung in German</u>	LP: Electrola E 83380/WCLP 781 LP: EMI 1C 147 29142-29143M CD: EMI CDM 769 6822
Munich January 1954	Munich RO Schmidt-Boelcke <u>Sung in German</u>	LP: Acanta DE 23.316-23.317/40.23528

Carmen, Excerpt (Parle-moi de ma mère)

Berlin September 1937	Perras Reichssender Orchestra Steiner <u>Sung in German</u>	Unpublished radio broadcast
Berlin April 1938	Rautawaara Städtische Oper Orchestra Schmidt-Isserstedt <u>Sung in German</u>	78: Telefunken E 2572 CD: Finlandia 588.152
Baden-Baden April 1952	Jurinac Südwestfunk Orchestra Ackermann <u>Sung in German</u>	LP: Acanta DE 23.316-23.317/40.23528
Munich January 1954	Schlemm Munich RO Schmidt-Boelcke <u>Sung in German</u>	Unpublished radio broadcast

JOHANNES BRAHMS (1833-1897)

Am Sonntagmorgen, zierlich angetan

Berlin   Raucheisen   LP: Acanta BB 23.124/40.23524
1942-1943

Botschaft (Wehe, Lüftchen, lind und lieblich)

Berlin   Raucheisen   LP: Acanta BB 23.124/40.23524
1942-1943   LP: Melodiya M10 41895-41896

Heimkehr (O brich' nicht, Steg!)

Berlin   Raucheisen   LP: Acanta BB 23.124/40.23524
1942-1943   LP: Melodiya M10 41895-41896

Heimweh I (Wie traulich war das Fleckchen)

Berlin   Raucheisen   45: DG EPL 30 523
1942-1943   LP: Acanta BB 23.124/40.23524
                                       CD: Berlin Classics BC 21672

Heimweh III (Ich sah als Knabe Blumen blüh'n)

Berlin   Raucheisen   LP: Acanta 40.23524
July 1943

Junge Lieder I (Meine Liebe ist grün)

Berlin   Raucheisen   LP: Acanta BB 23.124/40.23524
1942-1943

Der Kuss (Unter Blüten des Mai's)

Berlin   Raucheisen   45: DG EPL 30 523
February 1944   LP: Acanta BB 23.124/40.23524
                                       LP: Melodiya M10 41895-41896
                                       CD: Berlin Classics BC 21672

14 Anders

Brahms Lieder/concluded

Minnelied (Holder klingt der Vogelsang)

Berlin	Raucheisen	45: DG EPL 30 523
1942-1943		LP: Acanta BB 23.124/40.23524
		CD: Berlin Classics BC 21672

O liebliche Wangen, ihr macht mir Verlangen!

Berlin	Raucheisen	LP: Acanta BB 23.124/40.23524
1942-1943		

Sehnsucht (Hinter jenen dichten Wäldern)

Berlin	Raucheisen	45: DG EPL 30 523
1942-1943		LP: Acanta BB 23.124/40.23524
		LP: Melodiya M10 41895-41896
		CD: Berlin Classics BC 21672

Tambourliedchen (Den Wirbel schlag' ich gar so stark)

Berlin	Raucheisen	LP: Acanta BB 23.124/40.23524
1942-1943		

Ein Wanderer (Hier, wo sich die Strassen scheiden)

Berlin	Raucheisen	LP: Acanta BB 23.124/40.23524
1942-1943		

Wir wandelten, wir zwei zusammen

Berlin	Raucheisen	45: DG EPL 30 523
1942-1943		LP: Acanta BB 23.124
		CD: Berlin Classics BC 21672

Brahms Lieder sung by Anders also appear on Eterna LPs 820 443/822 610; 10 Brahms Lieder recorded for WDR Cologne with Weissenborn in October 1948 and tapes subsequently destroyed

EUGEN D'ALBERT (1864-1932)

Tiefland, Querschnitt

Berlin August 1935	Gura, Spletter, Nissen Städtische Oper Chorus BPO Schmidt-Isserstedt	78: Telefunken E 1873

GAETONO DONIZETTI (1797-1848)

Don Pasquale

Stuttgart February 1938	Role of Ernesto Perras, Hann, Schellenberg Reichssender Orchestra & Chorus Görlich Sung in German	Unpublished radio broadcast

L'elisir d'amore, Excerpt (Una furtiva lagrima)

Berlin January 1942	Städtische Oper Orchestra Lutze Sung in German	78: Telefunken E 3228 LP: Telefunken HT 2/KT 11007
Berlin 1942	Berlin RO Marszalek	LP: DG LPE 17 201/88 018 LP: Eterna 720 067 LP: BASF 22 21491-7
Berlin 1943	Städtische Oper Orchestra Grüber Sung in German	LP: DG LPEM 19 390/2721 212/2548 155 LP: Acanta 40.23528

16 Anders

NICO DOSTAL (1891-1981)

Die Flucht ins Glück, Excerpt (Meines Herzens brennende Sehnsucht)

Berlin	Städtische Oper	78: Telefunken E 3131
December 1940	Orchestra	LP: Telefunken HTP 515/NT 425
	Hühn	

EDMUND EYSLER (1874-1949)

Bruder Straubinger, Excerpt (Küssen ist keine Sünd')

Berlin	Städtische Oper	78: Telefunken A 1925
February 1936	Orchestra	LP: Telefunken HTP 515/NT 425/TS 3141/
		DP 628.636
Baden-Baden	Südwestfunk	45: Electrola E 50578
July 1951	Orchestra	LP: EMI 1C 147 29142-29143M
	Burkhard	

LEO FALL (1873-1925)

Madame Pompadour, Excerpt (Ein intimes Souper)

Cologne	Losch	LP: Electrola E 83740
January 1952	WDR Orchestra	LP: EMI 1C 147 29142-29143M
	Marszalek	LP: RCA VL 30319

Madame Pompadour, Excerpt (Ich bin dein Untertan)

Cologne	Losch	LP: Electrola E 83740
January 1952	WDR Orchestra	LP: EMI 1C 147 29142-29143M
	Marszalek	LP: RCA VL 30319
		CD: Acanta 43.812

Und der Himmel hängt voller Geigen, Potpourri from operettas by Fall

Cologne	Rothenberger,	78: Polydor HM 58 604
February 1952	Kellner, Thoms,	45: Polydor EPH 20 032
	W.Schneider,	LP: Polydor LPH 45 022
	W.Hofmann	
	WDR Orchestra	
	and Chorus	
	Marszalek	

LOUIS FERDINAND OF PRUSSIA (Born 1907)

8 Lieder: Stille; Vorgefühl; Der Heimatlose; Musikantengruss; An die Leserin; Der Tote spricht; Dank; Liebesbotschaft

1951	Koschnick	LP: Telefunken LSK 7028
		<u>Excerpts</u>
		45: Telefunken UV 258
		<u>LSK 7028 was a private edition for charity purposes</u>

FRIEDRICH VON FLOTOW (1812-1883)

Martha

Berlin October 1944	Role of Lyonel Berger, Tegethoff, Fuchs, Greindl, Sauer Staatskapelle and Chorus Schüler	LP: Urania URLP 217 LP: DG LPEM 19 253-19 254 LP: Eterna 820 243-820 244 LP: Acanta DE 21997 CD: Sonia 74805-74806 CD: Berlin Classics BC 21632 Excerpts LP: DG LPE 17 201/LPEM 19 390/88018/ 2548 155/2721 212 LP: Eterna 720 067 LP: BASF 22 21491-7 CD: Acanta 43.268

Martha, Querschnitt

Berlin 1936	Spletter, Tegethoff, Nissen Städtische Oper Orchestra & Chorus Schmidt-Isserstedt	78: Telefunken E 2060

Martha, Excerpt (Ach so fromm)

Berlin September 1937	Städtische Oper Orchestra Schüler	78: Telefunken A 2466 LP: Telefunken HT 29/TW 30054/AJ642.232 CD: Teldec 4509 955122
Cologne June 1937	Orchestra Kühn	Unpublished radio broadcast
Hannover June 1937	Niedersächsisches Staatsorchester Ebel von Sosen	Unpublished radio broadcast

UMBERTO GIORDANO (1867-1948)

Andrea Chenier, Excerpts (Un dì all' azzurro spazio; Come un bel dì di maggio)

Berlin January 1949	RIAS-Unterhaltungs- orchester Gaebel Sung in German	LP: Acanta DE 23.316-23.317/40.23528
Berlin 1954	RIAS-Unterhaltungs- orchester Gaebel Sung in German	DG unpublished

Andrea Chenier, Excerpt (Vicino a te)

Berlin January 1949	Musial RIAS-Unterhaltungs- orchester Gaebel Sung in German	LP: Acanta DE 23.316-23.317/40.23528

WALTER GOETZE (1883-1961)

Francesca da Rimini

Munich October 1937	Role of Paolo Martensen, Fiedler, Capellmann Reichssender Orchestra Winter	Unpublished radio broadcast

Liebe im Dreiklang

Cologne June 1951	Hübener, Zillger, W.Hofmann, W.Schneider WDR Chorus WDR Unterhaltungs- orchester Marszalek	Unpublished radio broadcast Excerpts LP: Electrola E 83740 LP: RCA VL 30319/VL 30373 CD: Acanta 43.812

RICHARD HEUBERGER (1850-1914)

Der Opernball, Excerpt (Im chambre séparée)

Cologne May 1954	Streich WDR Orchestra Marszalek	78: Polydor HM 49 260 45: Polydor EPH 20 153/NH 22 260 LP: Polydor LPH 45064/LPH 46 757/ LPHE 40 064/2430 243 CD: DG 447 6832

ENGELBERT HUMPERDINCK (1854-1921)

Königskinder

Cologne November 1952	Role of Königssohn Möller-Siepermann, Ihme-Sabisch, Fischer-Dieskau, Ollendorff WDR Orchestra and Chorus Kraus	LP: Ed Smith EJS 567 Incorrectly dated 1953

CHARLES GOUNOD (1818-1893)

Faust, Excerpt (Salut demeure)

Berlin April 1938	Städtische Oper Orchestra Lutze Sung in German	78: Telefunken E 2523 LP: Telefunken HT 2/KT 11007

EMMERICH KALMAN (1882-1953)

Die Csardasfürstin, Querschnitt

Berlin October 1934	Rautawaara Staatsoper Chorus BPO	78: Telefunken E 1690 LP: Telefunken HTP 516/TS 3141
Berlin March 1950	Schlemm, Mora Schöneberger Sängerknaben RIAS-Unterhaltungs- orchester Eisbrenner	Unpublished radio broadcast Excerpt LP: RCA VL 30319

Gräfin Maritza, Excerpt (Grüss' mir mein Wien!)

Berlin February 1936	Städtische Oper Orchestra	78: Telefunken A 1936 LP: Telefunken HT 9/TS 3141
Berlin November 1949	Orchestra Seidler-Winkler	78: Electrola EG 7378 45: Electrola E 20061 LP: EMI 1C 147 29142-29143M CD: EMI CDM 769 6822
Baden-Baden July 1951	Südwestfunk Orchestra Burkhard	LP: RCA VL 30319 CD: Acanta 43.812

Gräfin Maritza, Excerpt (Sag ja, mein Lieb, sag ja!)

Cologne 1954	Schlemm WDR Orchestra Marszalek	CD: Acanta 43.812

Gräfin Maritza, Excerpt (Einmal möchte ich wieder tanzen)

Cologne 1954	Schlemm WDR Orchestra Marszalek	LP: Polydor 249 136 CD: DG 447 6832

Gräfin Maritza, Excerpt (Komm Czigany!)

Cologne 1954	WDR Orchestra Marszalek	LP: Polydor 249 136 CD: Acanta 43.812 CD: DG 447 6832

Die Zirkusprinzessin, Excerpt (Zwei Märchenaugen)

Berlin January 1951	Staatskapelle Eisbrenner	78: Electrola EH 1359 LP: Electrola E 60006 LP: EMI 1C 147 29142-29143M CD: EMI CDM 769 6822
Baden-Baden July 1951	Südwestfunk Orchestra Burkhard	LP: RCA VL 30319 CD: Acanta 43.812

Damals in Budapest, Potpourri from Kalman operettas

Cologne 1953	Schörg, Möller-Siepermann, Fehringer, W.Hofmann, Wendland Sunshine-Quartett Cornel-Trio WDR Orchestra Marszalek	78: Polydor HM 58 621 45: Polydor EPH 20 037 LP: Polydor LPH 45 053

RUDOLF KATTNIGG (1895-1955)

Balkanliebe, Excerpt (Leise erklingen Glocken von Campanile)

Munich April 1953	Munich RO Schmidt-Boelcke	CD: Acanta 43.812

WILHELM KIENZL (1857-1941)

Der Evangelimann, Excerpt (Selig sind, die Verfolgung leiden)

Berlin April 1938	Städtische Oper Orchestra & Chorus Lutze	78: Telefunken E 2523 LP: Telefunken HT 2/KT 11007 CD: Teldec 4509 955122
Baden-Baden April 1952	Südwestfunk Orchestra Ackermann	LP: Acanta 40.23528 CD: Acanta 43.268

EDUARD KUENNECKE (1885-1953)

Der Vetter aus Dingsda, Excerpt (Ich bin nur ein armer Wandergesell')

Berlin November 1935	Städtische Oper Orchestra Schultze	78: Telefunken A 1901 LP: Telefunken HT 9/TS 3141/DP 628.636
Cologne January 1953	WDR Orchestra Marszalek	78: Polydor HM 48 927 45: Polydor EPH 20 121/NH 22 031 LP: Polydor LPH 45 064/LPH 46 757/2430243 LP: DG 2721 212 CD: DG 447 6832

FRANZ LEHAR (1870-1948)

Frasquita, Excerpt (Hab' ein blaues Himmelbett)

Cologne December 1952	WDR Orchestra Marszalek	78: Polydor HM 49 112 45: Polydor EPH 20 121/NH 22 112 LP: Polydor LPH 45 064/LPH 46 757/ LPHE 40 064/2430 243 LP: DG 2721 212 CD: DG 447 6832

Friederike, Excerpt (Sah ein Knab' ein Röslein)

Berlin January 1949	RIAS-Unterhaltungs- orchester Gaebel	LP: Polydor 249 136 LP: RCA VL 30319

Friederike, Excerpt (O Mädchen, mein Mädchen!)

Berlin January 1939	Städtische Oper Orchestra Hühn	78: Telefunken E 2830 LP: Telefunken HTP 515/NT 425/TS 3141/ DP 628.636
Berlin January 1949	RIAS-Unterhaltungs- orchester Gaebel	LP: Polydor 249 136 LP: RCA VL 30319 CD: Acanta 43.812 CD: DG 447 6832

Der Graf von Luxemburg, Excerpt (Bist du's, lachendes Glück!)

Berlin August 1934	Orchester Bund	78: Telefunken A 1675 LP: Telefunken HTP 515/NT 425/DP 628.636

Giuditta, Excerpt (Freunde, das Leben ist lebenswert!)

Berlin November 1934	Städtische Oper Orchestra Schmidt-Isserstedt	78: Telefunken A 1737 LP: Telefunken HT 9/NT 425/TS 3141/ DP 628.636

Giuditta, Excerpt (Du bist meine Sonne!)

Berlin	Städtische Oper	78: Telefunken A 1737
November 1934	Orchestra	LP: Telefunken HT 9/NT 425/TS 3141
	Schmidt-Isserstedt	

Das Land des Lächelns

Cologne	Role of Sou-Chong	LP: Karussell 109 520-109 521
April 1950	Eipperle,	Excerpts
	Rothenberger,	78: Polydor HM 58 607
	W.Hofmann	45: Polydor EPH 20 061
	WDR Orchestra	45: Royale EP 243
	and Chorus	LP: Polydor LPH 45 020/LPH 46 757/
	Marszalek	LPHE 40 064/LPHM 46 664/249 136/ 2430 243
		LP: Varsity 6991
		LP: Allegro 3066
		LP: Electrola E 83740
		LP: EMI 1C 147 29142-29143M
		LP: DG 2721 212/478 107
		LP: RCA VL 30319
		CD: Acanta 43.268
		CD: DG 447 6832

Das Land des Lächelns, Excerpt (Dein ist mein ganzes Herz)

Berlin	Staatskapelle	78: Electrola EH 1364
January 1951	Eisbrenner	LP: Electrola E 60006
		LP: EMI 1C 147 29142-29143M
		CD: EMI CDM 769 6822

Das Land des Lächelns, Excerpt (Immer nur lächeln)

Berlin	Staatskapelle	78: Electrola EH 1364
January 1951	Eisbrenner	LP: Electrola E 60006
		CD: EMI CDM 769 6822
Baden-Baden	Südwestfunk	LP: RCA VL 30319
July 1951	Orchestra	CD: Acanta 43.812
	Burkhard	

26 Anders

Das Land des Lächelns, Excerpt (Von Apfelblüten einen Kranz)

Berlin January 1939	Städtische Oper Orchestra Hühn	78: Telefunken E 2830 LP: Telefunken HT 9/NT 425/TS 3141/ DP 628.636
Munich January 1954	Munich RO Schmidt-Boelcke	Unpublished radio broadcast

Das Land des Lächelns, Excerpt (Wer hat die Liebe uns ins Herz gesenkt?)

Berlin May 1942	Rautawaara Städtische Oper Orchestra Lutze	78: Telefunken E 3306 LP: Telefunken HT 9
Baden-Baden July 1951	Tüscher Südwestfunk Orchestra Burkhard	LP: RCA VL 30319 CD: Acanta 43.812

Die lustige Witwe, Querschnitt

Berlin August 1935	Gura Städtische Oper Chorus BPO Schmidt-Isserstedt	78: Telefunken E 1866 LP: Telefunken HTP 517/TS 3141

Die lustige Witwe, Excerpt (Komm' in den kleinen Pavillon)

Berlin May 1942	Rautawaara Städtische Oper Orchestra Lutze	78: Telefunken E 3306 LP: Telefunken HT 9/NT 425

Paganini

Cologne January 1952	Role of Paganini Schlemm, Losch, Gehly, W.Hofmann, W.Schneider WDR Orchestra and Chorus Marszalek	LP: RCA VL 30314 LP: Acanta 22.482 CD: Acanta 43.810 Excerpts 78: Polydor HM 58 629 45: Polydor EPH 20 067 LP: Polydor LPH 45 067/LPH 46 757/ 249 136/2430 243 LP: Electrola E 83740 LP: DG 2721 212/478 107 LP: RCA VL 30319 CD: Acanta 43.812 CD: DG 447 6832

Paganini, Excerpt (Gern hab' ich die Frau'n geküsst)

Berlin December 1940	Städtische Oper Orchestra Hühn	78: Telefunken E 3131 LP: Telefunken HTP 515/TS 3141/DP 628.636

Paganini, Excerpt (Niemand liebt dich so wie ich)

Munich January 1954	Schlemm Munich RO Schmidt-Boelcke	Unpublished radio broadcast

Der Rastelbinder, Excerpt (Wenn zwei sich lieben)

Berlin April 1938	Rautawaara Städtische Oper Orchestra Schmidt-Isserstedt	78: Telefunken E 2572 LP: Telefunken HTP 515/NT 425

Schön ist die Welt, Excerpt (Schön ist die Welt)

Baden-Baden July 1951	Südwestfunk Orchestra Burkhard	LP: Electrola E 83740

Anders

Der Zarewitsch, Excerpt (Wolgalied)

Berlin	Staatskapelle	78: Electrola EH 1359
January 1951	Eisbrenner	LP: Electrola E 60006
		CD: EMI CDM 769 6822

Zigeunerliebe, Excerpt (Zorika, kehre züruck!)

Berlin	Orchestra	CD: EMI CDM 769 6822
November 1949	Seidler-Winkler	

Rendezvous mit Lehar, Potpourri

Berlin	Rautawaara	78: Telefunken E 1781
January 1935	BPO	LP: Telefunken HTP 517
	Schmidt-Isserstedt	

Peter Anders bei Franz Lehar, Potpourri

Berlin	Städtische Oper	78: Telefunken E 2400
November 1937	Orchestra	
	Lutze	

RUGGIERO LEONCAVALLO (1858-1919)

I Pagliacci, Querschnitt

Berlin 1936	Spletter, Schmitt-Walter Städtische Oper Orchestra & Chorus Schmidt-Isserstedt Sung in German	78: Telefunken E 2034

I Pagliacci, Excerpt (Un tal gioco)

Munich August 1953	Munich PO L.Ludwig Sung in German	78: DG LVM 62 913 45: DG EPL 30 012 LP: DG LPE 17 091

I Pagliacci, Excerpt (Vesti la giubba)

Berlin January 1939	Städtische Oper Orchestra Lutze Sung in German	78: Telefunken E 2816 LP: Telefunken JT 22/KT 11007
Munich 1953	Munich PO Hollreiser Sung in German	78: DG LVM 62 911 45: DG EPL 30 012 LP: DG LPE 17 091
Munich 1953	Munich PO Hollreiser	45: DG EPL 30 486/NL 32 025 LP: DG LPEM 19 390/2548 155/2721 212

I Pagliacci, Excerpt (No, Pagliacco non son!)

Berlin January 1939	Städtische Oper Orchestra Lutze Sung in German	78: Telefunken E 2816 LP: Telefunken HT 22/KT 11007
Munich 1953	Munich PO Hollreiser Sung in German	78: DG LVM 62 911 45: DG EPL 30 012

HAMBURGISCHE STAATSOPER
Intendant Dr. Günther Rennert

Sonnabend, den 3. Oktober 1953, 19.30 Uhr
Sonnabend-Abonnement (1. Folge)

FIDELIO

Oper in zwei Aufzügen (4 Bildern)
von Ludwig van Beethoven

Musikalische Leitung: Leopold Ludwig
Inszenierung: Günther Rennert
Bühnenbild und Kostüm: Alfred Siercke
Chöre: Günter Hertel

Don Fernando, Minister	James Pease
Don Pizarro, Gouverneur eines Staatsgefängnisses	Josef Metternich
Florestan, ein Gefangener	Peter Anders
Leonore, seine Gemahlin, unter dem Namen „Fidelio"	Birgit Nilsson a. G.
Rocco, Kerkermeister	Theo Herrmann
Marzelline, seine Tochter	Lore Hoffmann
Jacquino, Pförtner	Kurt Marschner
Erster Gefangener	Fritz Göllnitz
Zweiter Gefangener	Toni Blankenheim

Während der Verwandlung zum letzten Bild: 3. Leonoren-Ouvertüre

Im 4. Bild ist der Chor durch den Sonderchor der Hamburgischen Staatsoper verstärkt

Technische Leitung: Hermann Mendt

DEUTSCHE STAATSOPER

Montag, den 8. März 1954

OTHELLO

Oper in vier Akten von Arrigo Boito

Musik von Giuseppe Verdi

Musikalische Leitung: Wilhelm Loibner
Inszenierung: Michael Bohnen · Chöre: Karl Schmidt
Bühnenbild: Hainer Hill · Kostüme: Gisela Appelt

Othello, Mohr, Befehlshaber
    der venezianischen Flotte . . . . Peter Anders a. G.
Jago, Fähnrich . . . . Joseph Metternich a. G.
Cassio, Hauptmann . . . . Gerhard Stolze
Rodrigo, ein edler Venezianer . . . . Alwin Hendriks
Lodovico, Gesandter der Republik Venedig . . . . . . Gustav Köysti
Montano, der Vorgänger Othellos in der
    Statthalterei von Cypern . . . . Walter Großmann
Ein Herold . . . . Horst Jakob
Desdemona, Othellos Gemahlin . . . . Helma Prechter a. G.
Emilia, Jagos Gattin . . . . Adelheid Müller-Heß

Soldaten, Seeleute, Edeldamen und venezianische Nobile, Krieger, Volk

Ort: Eine Hafenstadt der Insel Cypern
Zeit: Ende des 15. Jahrhunderts

Technische Leitung: Max Hübner
Regie-Assistenz: Udo Esselun
Inspizient: Horst Wruck

32 Anders

CARL LOEWE (1796-1869)

Des Glockentürmers Töchterlein (Mein hochgebor'nes Schätzelein)

Berlin October 1944	Städtische Oper Orchestra Steinkopf	Unpublished radio broadcast
Berlin January 1945	Raucheisen	LP: Acanta 40.23534

ALBERT LORTZING (1801-1851)

Undine, Excerpt (Vater, Mutter, Schwestern, Brüder!)

Berlin September 1937	Städtische Oper Orchestra Schüler	78: Telefunken A 2405 LP: Telefunken HT 29/TW 30054/AJ642.232 CD: Teldec 4509 955122
Berlin 1943	Berlin RO Rother	LP: BASF 22 21491-7 LP: Acanta 40.23528 CD: Acanta 43.268
Cologne January 1952	WDR Orchestra Marszalek	LP: DG LPE 17 091/LPEM 19 390/2548 155/ 2721 212

Zar und Zimmermann, Excerpt (Leb' wohl, mein flandrisch Mädchen!)

Berlin September 1937	Städtische Oper Orchestra Schüler	78: Telefunken A 2405 LP: Telefunken HT 29/TW 30054/AJ642.232 CD: Teldec 4509 955122

HEINRICH MARSCHNER (1795-1861)

Der Sänger

Berlin January 1945	Raucheisen	LP: Acanta 40.23541

PIETRO MASCAGNI (1863-1945)

Cavalleria rusticana, Excerpt (No, no, Turiddu, rimani!)

Berlin February 1935	Rautawaara Städtische Oper Orchestra Schmidt-Isserstedt Sung in German	78: Telefunken E 1807 CD: Finlandia 588.152

Cavalleria rusticana, Excerpt (Viva il vino!)

Berlin February 1943	Städtische Oper Orchestra & Chorus Lutze Sung in German	78: Telefunken E 3338 LP: Telefunken HT 2/KT 11007
Munich April 1953	Munich Radio Orchestra & Chorus Schmidt-Boelcke Sung in German	Unpublished radio broadcast

Cavalleria rusticana, Excerpt (Mamma, quel vino è generoso!)

Berlin January 1942	Städtische Oper Orchestra Lutze Sung in German	78: Telefunken E 3228 LP: Telefunken HT 2/KT 11007

Der Bettelstudent, Excerpt (Nur das Eine bitt' ich dich)

Berlin	Rautawaara	78: Telefunken E 2629
April 1938	Städtische Oper	LP: Telefunken HT 9
	Orchestra	
	Schmidt-Isserstedt	

Der Bettelstudent, Excerpt (Ich setz' den Fall)

Berlin	Rautawaara	78: Telefunken E 2572
April 1938	Städtische Oper	LP: Telefunken HT 9
	Orchestra	
	Schmidt-Isserstedt	

<u>One aria from Der Bettelstudent also recorded in Cologne in June 1937 and conducted by Kühn</u>

Gasparone, Excerpt (Denk an dich, schwarze Ninetta!)

Cologne	WDR Orchestra	LP: Electrola E 83740
December 1949	Marszalek	LP: EMI 1C 147 29142-29143M

Gasparone, Excerpt (Nur Gold will ich haben)

Cologne	Schiebener	Unpublished radio broadcast
December 1949	WDR Orchestra	
	Marszalek	

Gasparone, Excerpt (O dass ich doch ein Räuber wär'!)

Cologne	WDR Orchestra	LP: Electrola E 83740
December 1949	Marszalek	LP: EMI 1C 147 29142-29143M
		LP: RCA VL 30319
		CD: Acanta 43.812

JULES MASSENET (1842-1912)

Manon, Excerpt (En fermant les yeux)

Munich	Munich PO	45: DG EPL 30 292
1954	Lehmann	LP: DG LPE 17 091/88 018
	Sung in German	

GIACOMO MEYERBEER (1791-1864)

L'Africaine, Excerpt (O Paradis!)

Cologne	WDR Orchestra	LP: DG LPE 17 091/LPEM 19 390/2548 155/
June 1951	Marszalek	2721 212
	Sung in German	LP: Acanta 40.23528

CARL MILLOECKER (1842-1899)

Der Bettelstudent, Querschnitt

Berlin	Spletter, Nissen	78: Telefunken E 2110
November 1936	Städtische Oper	LP: Telefunken HTP 516/TS 3141
	Orchestra & Chorus	
	Schultze	
Cologne	Streich, Witsch,	78: Polydor HM 58 615
1952	W.Schneider,	45: Polydor EPH 20 042
	Capellmann	LP: Polydor LPH 45 049/LPHM 46 664

Der Bettelstudent, Excerpt (Ich knüpfte manch zarte Bande)

Berlin	Städtische Oper	78: Telefunken A 2092
September 1936	Orchestra	LP: Telefunken HT 9/NT 425/DP 628.636

Der Bettelstudent, Excerpt (Ich hab' kein Geld, bin vogelfrei!)

Berlin	Städtische Oper	78: Telefunken A 2092
September 1936	Orchestra	LP: Telefunken HT 9/DP 628.636

36   Anders

WOLFGANG AMADEUS MOZART (1756-1791)

Cosl fan tutte, Excerpt (Un aura amorosa)

Hannover	Niedersächsisches	Unpublished radio broadcast
June 1937	Staatsorchester	
	Ebel von Sosen	
	Sung in German	

Don Giovanni, Excerpt (Dalla sua pace)

Berlin	Städtische Oper	78: Telefunken E 1796
February 1935	Orchestra	LP: Telefunken HT 29/TW 30062/LGM 65019/
	Schmidt-Isserstedt	AJ 642.232
	Sung in German	

Don Giovanni, Excerpt (Il mio tesoro)

Berlin	Städtische Oper	78: Telefunken E 1796
February 1935	Orchestra	LP: Telefunken HT 29/TW 30062/LGM 65019
	Schmidt-Isserstedt	AJ 642.232
	Sung in German	

Die Entführung aus dem Serail

Berlin	Role of Belmonte	Unpublished radio broadcast
July 1946	Berger, Streich,	Excerpts
	Schmidtmann,	LP: BASF 10 21495-8/10 22178-4/98 22176/
	L.Hofmann	22 21490-3/22 21491-7
	Staatskapelle	LP: Acanta BB 21495
	and Chorus	LP: Eterna 821 873
	Schmidt	CD: Acanta 43.268
		CD: Minerva MNA 21

Die Entführung aus dem Serail, Excerpt (O wie ängstlich!)

Berlin April 1935	Städtische Oper Orchestra Schmidt-Isserstedt	78: Telefunken E 1867 LP: Telefunken HT 29/TW 30062/LGM 65019/ 　　AJ 642.232 CD: Teldec 4509 955122
Munich December 1937	Reichssender Orchestra Winter	Unpublished radio broadcast
Berlin February 1945	Staatskapelle Heger	LP: DG LPE 17 201 LP: Eterna 720 067 LP: BASF 10.21495-8 LP: Acanta 40.23528 CD: Berlin Classics BC 21682

Die Entführung aus dem Serail, Excerpt (Hier soll ich dich denn sehen?)

Berlin May 1935	Städtische Oper Orchestra Schmidt-Isserstedt	78: Telefunken A 1874 78: Telefunken HT 29/TW 30062/LGM 65019/ 　　AJ 642.232 CD: Teldec 4509 955122
Berlin February 1945	Staatskapelle Heger	LP: DG LPE 17 201/LPEM 19 390/ 　　2548 155/2721 212 LP: Eterna 720 067 LP: BASF 10 21495-8/22 21491-7 CD: Acanta 43.268 CD: Berlin Classics BC 21682

Die Entführung aus dem Serail, Excerpt (Wenn der Freude Tränen fliessen)

Berlin February 1945	Staatskapelle Heger	LP: DG LPE 17 201/LPEM 19 390/ 　　2548 155/2721 212 LP: Eterna 720 067 LP: BASF 10 21495-8/22 21491-7 LP: Acanta 40.23528 CD: Acanta 43.268

Die Entführung aus dem Serail, Excerpt (Im Mohrenland gefangen)

Berlin May 1935	Städtische Oper Orchestra Schmidt-Isserstedt	78: Telefunken A 1874 LP: Telefunken HT 29/TW 30062/LGM 65019/ 　　AJ 642.232 CD: Teldec 4509 955122

38   Anders

La finta giardiniera

Hamburg January 1937	Role of Belfiore Engel, Schlee, Huxdorf, Stadelmaer Reichssender Orchestra & Chorus G.A.Schlemm Sung in German	Unpublished radio broadcast

Die Zauberflöte, Querschnitt

Berlin November 1936	Wulff, Hiller, Nissen Städtische Oper Orchestra & Chorus Schultze	78: Telefunken E 2133

Die Zauberflöte, Excerpt (Dies Bildnis ist bezaubernd schön)

Berlin April 1935	Städtische Oper Orchestra Schmidt-Isserstedt	78: Telefunken E 1867 LP: Telefunken HT 29/TW 30062/LGM 65019/ 　　AJ 642.232/DP 628.636 CD: Teldec 4509 955122
Berlin 1943	Städtische Oper Orchestra Grüber	LP: DG LPE 17 201/LPEM 19 390/88 018/ 　　2548 155/2721 212 LP: Eterna 720 067 LP: BASF 22 21491-7 LP: Acanta 40.23528 CD: Acanta 43.268 CD: Berlin Classics BC 21682

Die Zauberflöte, Excerpt (Soll ich dich, Teurer, nicht mehr seh'n?)

Berlin 1943	Eipperle, Hann Berlin RO Rother	LP: BASF 22 21491-7 CD: Acanta 43.268

OTTO NICOLAI (1810-1849)

Die lustigen Weiber von Windsor

Berlin August 1936	Role of Fenton Pfahl, Schilp, Nettesheim, Kandl, Hüsch, Windisch, E.Zimmermann Reichssender Orchestra & Chorus Steiner	Unpublished radio broadcast Performance mounted to mark the 1936 Olympic Games

Die lustigen Weiber von Windsor, Excerpt (Horch', die Lerche singt im Hain!)

Berlin November 1937	Städtische Oper Orchestra Schüler	78: Telefunken A 2466 LP: Telefunken HT 29/TW 30054/AJ642.232 CD: Teldec 4509 955122
Munich December 1937	Reichssender Orchestra Winter	Unpublished radio broadcast
Berlin January 1943	Staatskapelle Schüler	LP: DG LPE 17 201/88 018 LP: Eterna 720 067 LP: BASF 22 21491-7 LP: Acanta 40.23528 CD: Acanta 43.268 CD: Berlin Classics BC 21682

Abschied

Berlin October- November 1942	Raucheisen	LP: Acanta BB 23.124/40.23542

An die Entfernte

Berlin October 1942	Raucheisen Kniestädt-Quartett	LP: Acanta BB 23.124/40.23542 LP: Melodiya M10 41895-41896

Beruhigung

Berlin October- November 1942	Raucheisen	LP: Acanta BB 23.124/40.23542

40 Anders

Nicolai Lieder/concluded

Der getreue Bub

| Berlin | Raucheisen | LP: Acanta BB 23.124/40.23542 |
| October 1942 | Kniestädt-Quartett | LP: Melodiya M10 41895-41896 |

Liebesrausch

Berlin	Raucheisen	LP: Acanta BB 23.124/40.23542
October-		LP: Melodiya M10 41895-41896
November 1942		

Männersinn

Berlin	Raucheisen	LP: Acanta BB 23.124/40.23542
October-		
November 1942		

Rondino

Berlin	Raucheisen	LP: Acanta 40.23542
October-		LP: Melodiya M10 41895-41896
November 1942		

Der Schäfer im Mai

Berlin	Raucheisen	LP: Acanta BB 23.124/40.23542
October-		LP: Melodiya M10 41895-41896
November 1942		

Die Träne

Berlin	Raucheisen	LP: Acanta BB 23.124/40.23542
October-		LP: Melodiya M10 41895-41896
November 1942		

Wanderlied

| Berlin | Raucheisen | LP: Acanta BB 23.124/40.23542 |
| October 1942 | Kniestädt-Quartett | LP: Melodiya M10 41895-41896 |

JACQUES OFFENBACH (1819-1880)

Les contes d'Hoffmann

Berlin July 1946	Role of Hoffmann Berger, Streich, I.Klein, Prohaska Berlin Radio Orchestra & Chorus Rother Sung in German	LP: Urania URLP 224 LP: Gramophone (USA) 20154-20156 LP: Royale 1269-1271 LP: BASF 22 21804-2 LP: Acanta 40.21804 Excerpts LP: Royale 1322 LP: Saga XID 2133 LP: Eterna 820 248 LP: BASF 22 21490-3/22 21491-7 CD: Berlin Classics BC 21682

HANS PFITZNER (1869-1949)

Mailied (Wie herrlich leuchtet mir die Natur)

Berlin December 1944	Raucheisen	LP: Rococo 1015 LP: Acanta 40.23532

Studentenfahrt (Die Jäger zieh'n in grünen Wald)

Berlin December 1944	Raucheisen	LP: Acanta 40.23532

Trauerlied

Berlin December 1944	Raucheisen	LP: Rococo 1015 LP: Acanta 40.23532

GIACOMO PUCCINI (1858-1924)

La Bohème, Extracts

Berlin	Eipperle, Güden,	LP: BASF 10 21496-6
July 1942	Windisch,	LP: Melodiya M10 40757-40758
	Domgraf-Fassbaender	Excerpts
	Berlin RO	LP: BASF 22 21491-7
	Steinkopf	LP: Acanta 40.23528/DE 23.316-23.317
	Sung in German	

La Bohème, Excerpt (Chi è là? Una donna?....to end of Act 1)

Berlin	Cebotari	LP: Urania URLP 7105
1944	Berlin RO	CD: Berlin Classics BC 21682
	Rother	Excerpts
	Sung in German	45: Spezial EP 8014/EP 8039
		45: DG EPL 30 535
		LP: DG LPEM 19 349/LPEM 19 390/ 2548 155/2721 212
		LP: Eterna 720 071
		LP: BASF 22 21491-7
		LP: Historia H 677-678
		LP: Acanta 40.23528

La Bohème, Excerpt (Che gelida manina)

Berlin	Städtische Oper	78: Telefunken E 2628
April 1938	Orchestra	LP: Telefunken HT 2/KT 11007/DP 628.636
	Lutze	
	Sung in German	

La Bohème, Excerpt (Dunque è proprio finita!)

Berlin	Cebotari	CD: Berlin Classics BC 21682
1944	Berlin RO	
	Rother	
	Sung in German	

La Bohème, Excerpt (Sono andati?)

Baden-Baden	Jurinac	LP: Acanta DE 23.316-23.317
April 1952	Südwestfunk	CD: EMI CDM 769 6822
	Orchestra	
	Ackermann	
	Sung in German	

La fanciulla del West, Excerpt (Ch' ella mi credea libero)

Berlin	BPO	78: Telefunken A 1478
August 1933	Reuss	LP: Telefunken HT 2/KT 11007
	Sung in German	
Berlin	Berlin RO	45: DG EPL 30 535
1944	Steinkopf	LP: BASF 22 21491-7
	Sung in German	LP: Acanta 40.23528

Madama Butterfly

Königsberg	Role of Pinkerton	Unpublished radio broadcast
May 1937	L.Hofmann/Ilitsch,	
	Heyer, Hartmann	
	Reichssender	
	Orchestra & Chorus	
	Brückner	
	Sung in German	

Madama Butterfly, Excerpt (Bimba dagli occhi)

Berlin	Rautawaara	78: Telefunken E 1853
April 1935	Städtische Oper	CD: Finlandia 588.152
	Orchestra	
	Schmidt-Isserstedt	
	Sung in German	
Baden-Baden	Jurinac	LP: Electrola E 83380/WCLP 781
April 1952	Südwestfunk	LP: EMI 1C 147 29142-29143M
	Orchestra	CD: EMI CDM 769 6822
	Ackermann	
	Sung in German	

Manon Lescaut, Excerpt (Donna non vidi mai)

Berlin	BPO	78: Telefunken A 1478
August 1933	Reuss	LP: Telefunken HT 2/KT 11007
	Sung in German	
Berlin	Berlin RO	45: DG EPL 30 535
1943	Rother	LP: DG LPEM 19 390/2548 155
	Sung in German	LP: BASF 22 21491-7
		LP: Acanta 40.23528

44 Anders

Il tabarro

Stuttgart January 1938	Role of Henri Ranczak, Waldenau, Ahlersmayer, Buchta, Wieter Reichssender Orchestra & Chorus Krauss Sung in German	LP: BASF 10 22365-5 Excerpts LP: BASF 22 21491-7

Tosca, Excerpt (Recondita armonia)

Berlin August 1937	Städtische Oper Orchestra Schmidt-Isserstedt Sung in German	78: Telefunken A 2360 LP: Telefunken HT 22/KT 11007/DP628.636
Berlin 1944	Berlin RO Marszalek	LP: Acanta DE 23.316-23.317/BB 23.119/ 40.23528

Tosca, Excerpt (E lucevan le stelle)

Berlin September 1937	Städtische Oper Orchestra Schüler Sung in German	78: Telefunken A 2360 LP: Telefunken HT 22/KT 11007
Berlin 1944	Berlin RO Marszalek	Unpublished radio broadcast

Tosca, Excerpt (Ah quegli occhi!)

Berlin April 1938	Rautawaara Städtische Oper Orchestra Schmidt-Isserstedt Sung in German	78: Telefunken E 2654 CD: Finlandia 588.152

Turandot, Excerpt (Non piangere Liù!)

Berlin	Städtische Oper	78: Telefunken A 1510
October 1933	Orchestra	LP: Telefunken HT 22/KT 11007
	Reuss	
	Sung in German	

Turandot, Excerpt (Nessun dorma)

Berlin	Städtische Oper	78: Telefunken A 1510
October 1933	Orchestra	LP: Telefunken HT 22/KT 11007
	Reuss	
	Sung in German	

FRED RAYMOND (1900-1954)

Maske in Blau, Excerpt (In dir hab' ich mein Glück gefunden)

Berlin	Städtische Oper	78: Telefunken A 2305
September 1937	Orchestra	LP: Telefunken HT 9/NT 425
	Schüler	

NIKOLAI RIMSKY-KORSAKOV (1844-1908)

Sadko, Excerpt (Song of the Indian Guest)

Berlin	Städtische Oper	78: Telefunken A 2321
September 1937	Orchestra	LP: Telefunken HT 29/TW 30054/DP628.636
	Schüler	
	Sung in German	

46 Anders

MAX VON SCHILLINGS (1868-1933)

Glockenlieder, Song cycle

Berlin May 1943	Staatskapelle Heger	LP: Urania URLP 7104 LP: DG LPE 17 202 LP: Eterna 720 068 LP: Acanta BB 23.185 CD: Acanta 43.275 CD: Berlin Classics BC 21682

FRANZ SCHUBERT (1797-1828)

Die schöne Müllerin, Song cycle

Berlin 1947	Puchelt	Unpublished radio broadcast <u>Tapes probably destroyed</u>

Winterreise, Song cycle

Berlin February- March 1945	Raucheisen	LP: E-Collection (USA) 29312 LP: DG 89 574-89 575 LP: Eterna 820 193-820 194 LP: Melodiya M10 41779-41782
Cologne October 1948	Weissenborn	LP: Acanta DE 23.056/40.23056

Abschied/Schwanengesang (Ade, du munt're, du fröhliche Stadt!)

Berlin January 1943	Raucheisen	LP: DG 89 574-89 575 LP: Melodiya M10 41779-41782 CD: Acanta 44.2115-44.2117 CD: Berlin Classics BC 21662 <u>October 1944 has also been given as the</u> <u>recording date for this song</u>

Auf dem See (Und frische Nahrung, neues Blut)

Berlin June 1943	Raucheisen	LP: Melodiya M10 46681 005

Schubert Lieder/continued

Auf dem Strom (Nimm die letzten Abschiedsküsse)

Berlin	Raucheisen	LP: Melodiya M10 46681 005
April 1943	H.Berger, horn	

Aufenthalt/Schwanengesang (Rauschender Strom, brausender Wald)

Berlin	Raucheisen	LP: Melodiya M10 41779-41782
January 1943		CD: Acanta 44.2115-44.2117

Der Einsame (Wann meine Grillen schwirren)

Berlin	Raucheisen	LP: DG LPE 17 204/88 018/2721 212
1943		CD: Berlin Classics BC 21662

Einsamkeit (Gib' mir die Fülle der Einsamkeit!)

Berlin	Raucheisen	LP: Acanta DE 23.056/40.23056
1942		LP: Melodiya M10 41893-41894

Die Erwartung (Hör' ich das Pförtchen nicht gehen?)

Berlin	Raucheisen	Unpublished radio broadcast
November 1944		

Das Fischermädchen/Schwanengesang (Du schönes Fischermädchen)

Berlin	Raucheisen	Unpublished radio broadcast
1943		

Frühlingsglaube (Die linden Düfte sind erwacht)

Stuttgart	Giesen	LP: Telefunken HT 33/DP628.636/DP648.064
March 1947		

48 Anders

Schubert Lieder/continued

Frühlingssehnsucht/Schwanengesang (Säuselnde Lüfte wehend so mild)

Berlin January 1943	Raucheisen	LP: DG LPE 17 203/2721 212/89574-89575 LP: Melodiya M10 41779-41782 CD: Acanta 44.2115-44.2117 CD: Berlin Classics BC 21662 <u>October 1944 has also been given as the recording date for this song</u>

Ganymed (Wie im Morgenglanze du rings mich anglühst)

Berlin December 1942	Raucheisen	Unpublished radio broadcast
Stuttgart March 1947	Giesen	LP: Telefunken HT 33

Das Geheimnis (Sie konnte mir kein Wörtchen sagen)

Berlin May 1944	Raucheisen	LP: Melodiya M10 46681 005 CD: Berlin Classics BC 21662

Das gestörte Glück (Ich hab' ein heisses junges Blut)

Berlin 1943	Raucheisen	45: DG EPL 30 523 LP: DG 88 018 CD: Berlin Classics BC 21662

Das Heimweh (Oft in einsam stillen Stunden)

Berlin February 1944	Raucheisen	45: DG EPL 30 528 CD: Berlin Classics BC 21662

Im Frühling (Still sitz' ich an des Hügels Hang)

Berlin 1943	Raucheisen	LP: DG LPE 17 203 CD: Berlin Classics BC 21662

Schubert Lieder/continued

In der Ferne/Schwanengesang (Wehe den Fliehenden, Welt Hinausziehenden!)

Berlin	Raucheisen	45: DG EPL 30 528
January 1943		LP: DG 89 574-89 575
		LP: Melodiya M10 41779-41782
		CD: Acanta 44.2115-44.2117
		CD: Berlin Classics BC 21662

October 1944 has also been given as the recording date for this song

Der Jäger/Die schöne Müllerin (Was sucht denn der Jäger am Mühlbach hier?)

Berlin   Raucheisen   LP: DG 88 018
April 1943

Other version of this song included in the complete cycle of Schöne Müllerin listed above

Jägers Abendlied (Im Felde schleich' ich, still und wild)

Berlin   Raucheisen   LP: Melodiya M10 46681 005
1943

Kriegers Ahnung/Schwanengesang (In tiefer Ruh' liegt um mich her)

Berlin	Raucheisen	LP: DG LPE 17 204/89 574-89 575
October 1944		LP: Melodiya M10 41779-41782
		CD: Acanta 44.2115-44.2117
		CD: Berlin Classics BC 21662

Liebesbotschaft/Schwanengesang (Rauschendes Bächlein so silbern und hell)

Berlin	Raucheisen	45: DG EPL 30 528
January 1943		LP: DG 89 574-89 575/2721 212
		LP: Melodiya M10 41779-41782
		CD: Acanta 44.2115-44.2117
		CD: Berlin Classics BC 21662
Stuttgart	Giesen	LP: Telefunken HT 33/DP 648.064
March 1947		

Schubert Lieder/continued

Lied eines Schiffers an den Dioskuren (Dioskuren, Zwillingsbrüder!)

Stuttgart March 1947	Giesen	LP: Telefunken HT 33/DP 648.064

Der Liedler (Gib', Schwester, mir die Harf' herab!)

Berlin 1943	Raucheisen	LP: DG LPE 17 203 LP: Melodiya M10 46681 005 CD: Berlin Classics BC 21662

Der Musensohn (Durch Feld und Wald zu schweifen)

Berlin 1943	Raucheisen	LP: Melodiya M10 46681 005
Stuttgart March 1947	Giesen	LP: Telefunken HT 33/DP 648.064

Nacht und Träume (Heil'ge Nacht, du sinkest nieder)

Stuttgart March 1947	Giesen	LP: Telefunken HT 33/DP628.636/DP648.064

Der Sänger (Was hör' ich draussen vor dem Tor?)

Berlin 1943	Raucheisen	Unpublished radio broadcast

Der Schiffer (Friedlich lieg' ich hingegossen)

Berlin January 1944	Raucheisen	LP: Melodiya M10 46681 005

Schwanengesang (Wie klag' ich's aus, das Sterbegefühl?)

Berlin January 1943	Raucheisen	Unpublished radio broadcast

Schubert Lieder/concluded

Ständchen (Horch', horch', die Lerch'!)

Berlin May 1944	Raucheisen	LP: DG LPE 17 203 CD: Berlin Classics BC 21662

Ständchen/Schwanengesang (Leise flehen meine Lieder)

Berlin January 1943	Raucheisen	LP: DG LPE 17 203/89 574-89 575 LP: Melodiya M10 41779-41782 CD: Acanta 44.2115-44.2117 CD: Berlin Classics BC 21662
Cologne June 1954	Weissenborn	Unpublished radio broadcast

Die Taubenpost/Schwanengesang (Ich hab' eine Brieftaub' in meinem Sold)

Berlin October 1943	Raucheisen	LP: DG LPE 17 204 LP: Rococo 1015 LP: Melodiya M10 41779-41782 CD: Acanta 44.2115-44.2117 CD: Berlin Classics BC 21662

Trockne Blumen/Die schöne Müllerin (Ihr Blümlein alle, die sie mir gab)

Berlin April 1943	Raucheisen	LP: Melodiya M10 46681 005

Other version of this song in the complete cycle of Schöne Müllerin listed above

Wohin?/Die schöne Müllerin (Ich hört' ein Bächlein rauschen)

Stuttgart March 1947	Giesen	LP: Telefunken HT 33/DP628.636/DP648.064

Other version of this song in the complete cycle of Schöne Müllerin listed above

Schubert Lieder sung by Anders also appear on Eterna LPs 820 442/820 443/ 820 444/822 611; 4 Schubert Lieder recorded with Weissenborn in Cologne in May 1948 and tapes subsequently destroyed; 5 Schubert Lieder (Schwanengesang) recorded with Weissenborn in October 1948 and tapes subsequently destroyed

ROBERT SCHUMANN (1810-1856)

Dichterliebe, Song cycle

Bremen 1947	Weissenborn	Unpublished radio broadcast

An den Sonnenschein (O Sonnenschein, wie scheinst du mir ins Herz hinein!)

Berlin January 1945	Raucheisen	Unpublished radio broadcast

Die beiden Grenadiere (Nach Frankreich zogen zwei Grenadier')

Stuttgart April 1949	Giesen	LP: Telefunken HT 33/DP 648.064

Familiengemälde (Grossvater und Grossmutter, die sassen im Gartenhag)

Berlin May 1944	Lemnitz Raucheisen	45: DG EPL 30 524 LP: Saga XIG 8007 LP: Melodiya M10 41893-41894 CD: Berlin Classics BC 21672

Frühlingsfahrt (Es zogen zwei rüst'gen Gesellen)

Berlin February 1945	Städtische Oper Orchestra Steinkopf	Unpublished radio broadcast
Stuttgart April 1949	Giesen	LP: Telefunken HT 33/DP 648.064

Der Hidalgo (Es ist so süss zu scherzen)

Berlin May 1943	Raucheisen	LP: Rococo 1015 LP: Melodiya M10 41893-41894
April 1948	Weissenborn	78: Electrola DA 5503 LP: Electrola E 83380/WCLP 781

Schumann Lieder/continued

Intermezzo/Liederkreis op 39 (Dein Bildnis wunderselig)

Stuttgart April 1949	Giesen	LP: Telefunken HT 33/DP628.636/DP648.064

Lorelei (Es flüstern und rauschen die Wogen)

Berlin June 1943	Raucheisen	LP: DG LPE 17 204/2721 212 CD: Berlin Classics BC 21672

Der Nussbaum (Es grünet ein Nussbaum vor dem Haus)

Berlin January 1943	Raucheisen	Unpublished radio broadcast

Provencalisches Lied (In den Talen der Provence)

Berlin May 1943	Raucheisen	LP: Rococo 1015 LP: Melodiya M10 41893-41894
April 1948	Weissenborn	78: Electrola DA 5503

Des Sängers Trost (Weint auch einst kein Liebchen)

Berlin 1943	Raucheisen	LP: DG LPE 17 204/88018/2721 212 CD: Berlin Classics BC 21672

Schöne Fremde/Liederkreis op 39 (Es rauschen die Wipfel und schauern)

Berlin January 1945	Raucheisen	Unpublished radio broadcast
Stuttgart April 1949	Giesen	LP: Telefunken HT 33/DP628.636/DP648.064

Die Sennin (Schöne Sennin noch einmal)

Berlin June 1943	Raucheisen	LP: DG LPE 17 204 CD: Berlin Classics BC 21672

54 Anders

Schumann Lieder/concluded

Sonntags am Rhein (Des Sonntags in der Morgenstund')

Berlin   Raucheisen   LP: Melodiya M10 41893-41894
May 1943

Stille Tränen (Du bist vom Schlaf erstanden)

Berlin   Raucheisen   LP: DG LPE 17 204/88 018
May 1943   CD: Berlin Classics BC 21672

Unterm Fenster (Wer ist vor meiner Kammertür?)

Berlin   Lemnitz   LP: Saga XIG 8007
May 1944   Raucheisen   LP: Melodiya M10 41893-41894

Wanderlied (Wohlauf! Noch getrunken den funkelnden Wein!)

Berlin   Raucheisen   LP: Melodiya M10 41893-41894
May 1943

Wiegenlied (Schlaf', Kindlein, schlaf'!)

Berlin   Lemnitz   LP: Saga XIG 8007
May 1944   LP: Melodiya M10 41893-41894

Zum Schluss/Myrthen (Hier in diesen erdbeklomm'nen Lüften)

Stuttgart   Giesen   LP: Telefunken HT 33/DP 648.064
April 1949

Schumann Lieder sung by Anders also appear on Eterna LPs 820 443/822 610; 11
Schumann Lieder recorded with Weissenborn in Cologne in October 1948 and tapes
subsequently destroyed

BEDRICH SMETANA (1824-1884)

The Bartered Bride, Excerpt (So I find you here!/My dearest love, now listen!)

Baden-Baden April 1952	Jurinac Südwestfunk Orchestra Ackermann Sung in German	LP: Electrola E 83380/WCLP 781 LP: EMI 1C 147 29142-29143M CD: EMI CDM 769 6822
Munich January 1954	Schlemm Munich RO Schmidt-Boelcke Sung in German	Unpublished radio broadcast

The Bartered Bride, Excerpt (Just listen to me for a moment!)

Berlin September 1940	Schirp Städtische Oper Orchestra Schmidt-Isserstedt Sung in German	78: Telefunken E 3214 LP: Telefunken HT 22/KT 11007 CD: Telefunken 4509 955122
Berlin March 1950	Hoppe RIAS-Unterhaltungs- orchester Gaebel Sung in German	Unpublished radio broadcast

The Bartered Bride, Excerpt (It must succeed!)

Berlin March 1950	RIAS-Unterhaltungs- orchester Gaebel Sung in German	DG unpublished DG has a recording date of 1954

The Bartered Bride, Excerpt (Now in happiness and grief)

Berlin March 1950	Harder RIAS-Unterhaltungs- orchester Gaebel Sung in German	Unpublished radio broadcast

ROBERT STOLZ (1880-1975)

Mein Herz ruft immer nur nach Dir

| Berlin | Orchestra | 78: Telefunken A 1641 |
| 1934 | Bund | |

Ob blond oder braun, ich lieb' alle Frau'n

Berlin	Städtische Oper	78: Telefunken A 1857
September 1935	Orchestra	LP: Telefunken HT 9/DP 628.636
	Schultze	

Schenk mir dein Herz heute nacht!

Berlin	Städtische Oper	78: Telefunken A 1857
September 1935	Orchestra	
	Schultze	

Zauber der Bohème, Excerpt (Ich liebe dich)

Berlin	Städtische Oper	78: Telefunken A 2305
September 1937	Orchestra	LP: Telefunken HT 9
	Schüler	

OSCAR STRAUS (1870-1954)

Ein Walzertraum, Excerpt (Da draussen im duftenden Garten)

| Berlin | Städtische Oper | 78: Telefunken A 1936 |
| February 1936 | Orchestra & Chorus | LP: Telefunken HTP 515/TS 3141 |

| Berlin | Orchestra | CD: EMI CDM 769 6822 |
| November 1949 | Seidler-Winkler | |

Alt-Wiener Reigen

Cologne	Losch	LP: Polydor 249 136
December 1950	WDR Orchestra	
	Marszalek	

JOHANN STRAUSS (1825-1899)

Die Fledermaus

Stuttgart February 1938	Role of Eisenstein Teschemacher, Wulf, Mikorey, Schmitt-Walter, Fiedler Reichssender Orchestra & Chorus Görlich	Unpublished radio broadcast
Berlin November 1949	Schlemm, Streich, Krebs, Brauer Berlin Radio Orchestra & Chorus Fricsay	CD: Melodram MEL 29001 CD: DG 447 3702 Excerpts LP: Melodram MEL 226

Die Fledermaus, Querschnitt

Berlin August 1933	Berger,E.Friedrich, C.Müller, Frind, Fuchs Städtische Oper Chorus BPO Reuss	78: Telefunken A 1456 LP: Telefunken HTP 516
Cologne 1952	Trötschel,Streich, W.Hofmann, W.Schneider WDR Orchestra and Chorus Marszalek	78: Polydor LM 58 612 45: Polydor EPH 20 038 LP: Polydor LPHM 46 664/LPH 45 025 Excerpts LP: Polydor LPHM 46 757/2430 243 CD: DG 447 6832

Karneval in Rom

Cologne December 1950	Role of Arthur Losch, Zillger, W.Schneider, Capellmann, W.Hofmann WDR Orchestra and Chorus Marszalek	Unpublished radio broadcast Excerpts LP: Electrola E 83740 LP: Polydor 249 136 LP: RCA VL 30312

Eine Nacht in Venedig, Querschnitt

Cologne May 1954	Streich, Weigelt Schulz, W. Hofmann WDR Orchestra and Chorus Marszalek	78: Polydor LM 58 626 45: Polydor EPH 20 052 LP: Polydor LPHM 46 664/LPH 45 067 <u>Excerpts</u> LP: Polydor LPHM 46 757/LPHE 40 064/ 2430 243 LP: DG 2721 212 LP: RCA VL 30319 CD: DG 447 6832

Eine Nacht in Venedig, Excerpt (Treu sein, das liegt mir nicht!)

Berlin May 1935	Städtische Oper Orchestra Schmidt-Isserstedt	78: Telefunken A 1834 LP: Telefunken HT 9/TS 3141
Cologne December 1950	WDR Orchestra Marszalek	LP: Polydor 249 136 CD: Acanta 43.812

Eine Nacht in Venedig, Excerpt (Komm in die Gondel!)

Berlin May 1935	Städtische Oper Orchestra Schmidt-Isserstedt	78: Telefunken A 1834 LP: Telefunken HT 9/NT 425/TS 3141
Berlin February 1951	Berlin RO Fricsay	LP: Melodram MEL 226

<u>An aria from Nacht in Venedig also recorded in Cologne in June 1937 with Reichssender Orchestra conducted by Kühn</u>

Der Zigeunerbaron, Querschnitt

Berlin April 1934	Gura Städtische Oper Orchestra & Chorus Reuss	78: Telefunken E 1673 LP: Telefunken HTP 517/TS 3141
Cologne 1952	Trötschel, Peter, Kusche WDR Orchestra and Chorus Marszalek	78: Polydor LM 58 613 45: Polydor EPH 20 050 LP: Polydor LPHM 46 664/LPH 45 025 <u>Excerpts</u> LP: Polydor LPHM 46 757/2430 243 LP: DG 2721 212

Der Zigeunerbaron, Excerpt (Als flotter Geist)

Berlin February 1951	Berlin RO Fricsay	LP: Melodram MEL 226
Baden-Baden July 1951	Südwestfunk Orchestra Burkhard	45: Electrola E 50578 LP: Electrola E 83740/E 83380/WCLP 781 CD: Acanta 43.812

Der Zigeunerbaron, Excerpt (Wer uns getraut)

Berlin April 1938	Rautawaara Städtische Oper Orchestra Schmidt-Isserstedt	78: Telefunken E 2629 LP: Telefunken HTP 515/DP 628.636
Berlin February 1951	Musial Berlin RO Fricsay	LP: Melodram MEL 226
Baden-Baden July 1951	Tüscher Südwestfunk Orchestra Burkhard	LP: RCA VL 30319 CD: Acanta 43.812
Cologne May 1954	Streich WDR Orchestra Marszalek	78: Polydor LM 49 260 45: Polydor NH 22 260 LP: Polydor LPHE 40 064 CD: DG 447 6832

RICHARD STRAUSS (1864-1949)

Ariadne auf Naxos

Edinburgh August 1950	Role of Bacchus Zadek, Hollweg, Springer, Cantelo, M.Thomas, Young, RPO Beecham	LP: Beecham Society WSA 511-512 Closing scene LP: Acanta DE 23.316-23.317

Daphne

Hamburg October 1949	Role of Apollo Cunitz, R.Fischer, Fehenberger, Greindl NDR Orchestra and Chorus Grüber	Unpublished radio broadcast

Der Rosenkavalier, Excerpt (Di rigori armato)

Berlin August 1937	Städtische Oper Orchestra Schmidt-Isserstedt	78: Telefunken A 2321 LP: Telefunken HT 29/TW 30054/DP628.636

Allerseelen (Stell' auf den Tisch die duftenden Reseden)

Berlin 1944-1945	Raucheisen	45: DG EPL 30 524 LP: Acanta 40.23546 CD: Berlin Classics BC 21672
Berlin May 1949	Weissenborn	Unpublished radio broadcast

Breit' über mein Haupt dein schwarzes Haar

Stuttgart April 1949	Giesen	LP: Telefunken HT 33
Berlin May 1949	Weissenborn	Unpublished radio broadcast

Cäcilie (Wenn du es wüsstest)

Berlin February 1945	Städtische Oper Orchestra Steinkopf	Unpublished radio broadcast
Berlin May 1949	Weissenborn	Unpublished radio broadcast
Cologne June 1954	Weissenborn	Unpublished radio broadcast
Munich 1954	Munich PO Lehmann	45: DG EPL 30 102/EPL 36 122 CD: DG 445 0592 <u>Anders' final recording sessions</u>

Die Georgine (Warum so spät erst, Georgine?)

Berlin 1944-1945	Raucheisen	LP: Acanta 40.23546
Stuttgart April 1949	Giesen	LP: Telefunken HT 33

62   Anders

Strauss Lieder/continued

Heimliche Aufforderung (Auf, hebe die funkelnde Schale empor zum Mund!)

Berlin September 1938	BPO Lutze	78: Telefunken A 2684 45: Telefunken UV 244 LP: Telefunken HT 36/DP 648.064
Berlin 1943	Städtische Oper Orchestra Keilberth	Unpublished radio broadcast
Berlin 1944-1945	Raucheisen	45: DG EPL 30 524 LP: Acanta 40.23546 CD: Berlin Classics BC 21672
Berlin February 1945	Städtische Oper Orchestra Steinkopf	Unpublished radio broadcast
Berlin 1949	Weissenborn	Unpublished radio broadcast
Cologne June 1954	Weissenborn	Unpublished radio broadcast
Munich 1954	Munich PO Lehmann	45: DG EPL 30 103/EPL 36 122 CD: DG 445 0592

Ich trage meine Minne

Berlin September 1938	BPO Lutze	78: Telefunken A 2782 45: Telefunken UV 244 LP: Telefunken HT 36/DP628.636/DP648.064
Berlin 1944-1945	Raucheisen	LP: Acanta 40.23546
Berlin 1944-1945	Berlin RO Rother	LP: Melodiya M10 41895-41896
Munich 1954	Munich PO Lehmann	45: DG EPL 30 103/EPL 36 122 CD: DG 445 0592 <u>Anders' final recording sessions</u>

Strauss Lieder/continued

Liebeshymnus (Heil jenem Tag!)

Berlin February 1942	BPO Furtwängler	LP: Melodiya M10 41233-41234 LP: French Furtwängler Society SWF 7906 LP: Discocorp IGI 382 LP: Arabesque AR 8082 LP: Nippon Columbia OZ 7603 LP: Cetra FE 41 CD: Priceless D 18355 CD: Arabesque Z 6082 CD: Seven Seas KICC 2111 CD: Melodiya MEL 10 00723 CD: Music and Arts CD 829
Berlin 1943	Städtische Oper Orchestra Keilberth	LP: Acanta BB 23.185
Cologne June 1954	Weissenborn	Unpublished radio broadcast

Morgen (Und morgen wird die Sonne wieder scheinen)

Berlin 1944-1945	Berlin RO Rother	LP: DG LPE 17 202 LP: Eterna 720 068 LP: Acanta BB 23.185 LP: Melodiya M10 41895-41896 CD: Berlin Classics BC 21682
Berlin January 1945	Raucheisen	Unpublished radio broadcast
April 1948	Weissenborn	78: Electrola DA 5504
Cologne June 1954	Weissenborn	Unpublished radio broadcast

Nachtgang (Wir gingen durch die stille milde Nacht)

Stuttgart April 1949	Giesen	LP: Telefunken HT 33

Strauss Lieder/continued

Nichts (Nennen soll ich, sagt ihr)

Berlin　　　　　　Weissenborn　　　　　Unpublished radio broadcast
May 1949

Ruhe meine Seele (Nicht ein Lüftchen regt sich leise)

Cologne　　　　　Weissenborn　　　　　Unpublished radio broadcast
June 1954

Ständchen (Mach' auf, mach' auf, doch leise, mein Kind!)

Berlin September 1938	BPO Lutze	78: Telefunken A 2684 45: Telefunken UV 244 LP: Telefunken HT 36/DP628.636/DP648.064
Berlin 1943	Städtische Oper Orchestra Keilberth	Unpublished radio broadcast
Berlin April 1944	Städtische Oper Orchestra Grüber	LP: Acanta BB 23.185
Berlin 1944-1945	Raucheisen	LP: Acanta 40.23546
Stuttgart April 1949	Giesen	Unpublished radio broadcast
Berlin May 1949	Weissenborn	Unpublished radio broadcast
Cologne June 1954	Weissenborn	Unpublished radio broadcast

Strauss Lieder/continued

Traum durch die Dämmerung (Weite Wiesen im Dämmergrau)

Berlin September 1938	BPO Lutze	78: Telefunken A 2782 45: Telefunken UV 244 LP: Telefunken HT 36/DP 648.064
Berlin 1944-1945	Berlin RO Rother	LP: Acanta BB 23.185 LP: Melodiya M10 41895-41896
Cologne June 1954	Weissenborn	Unpublished radio broadcast

Verführung (Der Tag, der schwüle, verblasst)

Berlin February 1942	BPO Furtwängler	LP: Melodiya M10 41233-41234 LP: French Furtwängler Society SWF 7906 LP: Discocorp IGI 382 LP: Arabesque AR 8082 LP: Nippon Columbia OZ 7603 LP: Cetra FE 41 CD: Priceless D 18355 CD: Arabesque Z 6082 CD: Seven Seas KICC 2111 CD: Melodiya MEL 10 00723 CD: Music and Arts CD 829
Berlin 1943	Städtische Oper Orchestra Keilberth	LP: Acanta BB 23.185

66 Anders

Strauss Lieder/continued

Waldseligkeit (Der Wald beginnt zu rauschen)

Berlin February 1942	BPO Furtwängler	LP: Melodiya M10 41233-41234 LP: French Furtwängler Society SWF 7906 LP: Discocorp IGI 382 LP: Arabesque AR 8082 LP: Nippon Columbia OZ 7603 LP: Cetra FE 41 CD: Priceless D 18355 CD: Arabesque Z 6082 CD: Seven Seas KICC 2111 CD: Melodiya MEL 10 00723 CD: Music and Arts CD 829
Berlin 1943	Städtische Oper Orchestra Keilberth	LP: Acanta BB 23.185

Winterliebe (Der Sonne entgegen in Liebesgluten)

Berlin February 1942	BPO Furtwängler	LP: Melodiya M10 41233-41234 LP: French Furtwängler Society SWF 7906 LP: Discocorp IGI 382 LP: Arabesque AR 8082 LP: Nippon Columbia OZ 7603 LP: Cetra FE 41 CD: Priceless D 18355 CD: Arabesque Z 6082 CD: Seven Seas KICC 2111 CD: Melodiya MEL 10 00723 CD: Music and Arts CD 829

Strauss Lieder/concluded

Zueignung (Ja, du weisst es, teure Seele!)

April 1948	Weissenborn	78: Electrola DA 5504 LP: Electrola E 83380/WCLP 781
Stuttgart April 1949	Giesen	Unpublished radio broadcast
Berlin May 1949	Weissenborn	Unpublished radio broadcast
Hamburg 1952	Beckmann	Unpublished radio broadcast
Cologne June 1954	Weissenborn	Unpublished radio broadcast
Munich 1954	Munich PO Lehmann	45: DG EPL 30 102/EPL 36 122 CD: DG 445 0592 Anders' final recording sessions

Strauss Lieder sung by Anders also appear on Eterna LPs 820 443/822 610; 10 Strauss Lieder also recorded with Weissenborn in Cologne in May 1948 and tapes subsequently destroyed; unspecified Strauss Lieder recorded with Weissenborn in Bremen in 1947

PIOTR TCHAIKOVSKY (1840-1893)

Evgeny Onegin, Excerpt (Faint echo of my youth)

Berlin   Städtische Oper   78: Telefunken E 1761
November 1934   Orchestra   LP: Telefunken HT 2/KT 11007/DP628.636
    Schmidt-Isserstedt
    Sung in German

Berlin   Staatskapelle   Unpublished video recording
August 1945   K.Schmidt   Recording incomplete; from re-opening of
    Sung in German   Deutsche Staatsoper in Admiralspalast

Yolantha

Berlin   Role of Vaudemont   Unpublished radio broadcast
April 1935   Cebotari, Böhme,   Tapes probably destroyed
    Nissen
    Funkorchester
    and Chorus
    Steiner
    Sung in German

Komponisten-Bildnis Tchaikovsky

Berlin   Gura, Stech   78: Telefunken E 1888
August 1935   BPO
    Schröder

As they kept on saying

Stuttgart   Giesen   LP: Telefunken HT 36/DP 648.064
April 1951   Sung in German

At the ball

Stuttgart   Giesen   LP: Telefunken HT 36/DP 648.064
April 1951   Sung in German

Tchaikovsky Songs/concluded

None but the lonely heart

Stuttgart	Giesen	LP: Telefunken HT 36/DP628.636/DP648.064
April 1951	Sung in German	

O sing that song!

Stuttgart	Giesen	LP: Telefunken HT 36/DP 648.064
April 1951	Sung in German	

Painfully and sweetly

Stuttgart	Giesen	LP: Telefunken HT 36/DP 648.064
April 1951	Sung in German	

Thy radiant image

Stuttgart	Giesen	LP: Telefunken HT 36/DP628.636/DP648.064
April 1951	Sung in German	

Why?

Stuttgart	Giesen	LP: Telefunken HT 36/DP 648.064
April 1951	Sung in German	

AMBROISE THOMAS (1811-1896)

Mignon, Querschnitt

Berlin	Gmeiner, Koegel,	78: Telefunken E 2043
1936	Nissen	
	Städtische Oper	
	Chorus	
	BPO	
	Schmidt-Isserstedt	
	Sung in German	

GIUSEPPE VERDI (1813-1901)

Aida, Excerpt (Celeste Aida)

Hannover June 1937	Niedersächsisches Staatsorchester Ebel von Sosen Sung in German	Unpublished radio broadcast
Berlin April 1938	Städtische Oper Orchestra Lutze Sung in German	78: Telefunken E 2628 LP: Telefunken HT 2/KT 11007
Cologne June 1951	WDR Orchestra Marszalek Sung in German	LP: DG LPE 17 091/LPEM 19 390/88018/ 2548 155/2721 212 LP: Acanta DE 23.316-23.317/40.23528

Otello

Berlin January 1951	Role of Otello Trötschel, Metternich Berlin Radio Orchestra & Chorus Fricsay Sung in German	Unpublished radio broadcast Excerpts only may have been preserved

Otello, Excerpt (Già nella notte densa)

Baden-Baden April 1952	Jurinac Südwestfunk Orchestra Ackermann Sung in German	LP: Electrola E 83380/WCLP 781 LP: EMI 1C 147 29142-29143M LP: Acanta DE 23.316-23.317/40.23528 CD: EMI CDM 769 6822

Rigoletto, Querschnitt

Berlin October 1933	Ruzicka,Tegethoff, Bischof, Reinmar Städtische Oper Orchestra & Chorus Reuss Sung in German	78: Telefunken E 1509

Rigoletto, Excerpt (Questa o quella)

Berlin	Städtische Oper	78: Telefunken A 2430
November 1937	Orchestra	LP: Telefunken HT 2/KT 11007
	Lutze	
	Sung in German	

Rigoletto, Excerpt (La donna è mobile)

Hannover	Niedersächsisches	Unpublished radio broadcast
June 1937	Staatsorchester	
	Ebel von Sosen	
	Sung in German	

Berlin	Städtische Oper	78: Telefunken A 2430
November 1937	Orchestra	LP: Telefunken HT 2/KT 11007/DP628.636
	Lutze	
	Sung in German	

La Traviata, Querschnitt

Berlin	Pfahl, Fuchs	78: Telefunken E 1733
November 1934	Staatsoper Chorus	
	Städtische Oper	
	Orchestra	
	Schmidt-Isserstedt	
	Sung in German	

La traviata, Act 3

Berlin	Trötschel,	Unpublished radio broadcast
January 1951	Metternich	
	Berlin Radio	
	Orchestra & Chorus	
	Fricsay	
	Sung in German	

La Traviata, Excerpt (De' miei bollenti spiriti)

Munich August 1953	Munich PO L.Ludwig Sung in German	78: DG LM 62 913 45: DG EPL 30 012 LP: DG LPE 17 091/LPEM 19 390/88 018/ 2548 155/2721 212
Munich August 1953	Munich PO L.Ludwig	45: DG EPL 30 486/NL 32 025

La Traviata, Excerpt (Parigi o cara)

Berlin October 1953	Berger BPO Rother Sung in German	DG unpublished Not an Electrola recording as stated in Erna Berger discography(Teachers & pupils)
Berlin October 1953	Berger BPO Rother	DG unpublished Not an Electrola recording as stated in Erna Berger discography(Teachers & pupils)

Il trovatore, Querschnitt

Berlin November 1934	Rautawaara, Klose, Fuchs Städtische Oper Chorus BPO Schmidt-Isserstedt Sung in German	78: Telefunken E 1715

Il trovatore, Excerpt (Di quella pira!)

Berlin February 1943	Städtische Oper Orchestra & Chorus Lutze Sung in German	78: Telefunken E 3338 LP: Telefunken HT 22/KT 11007

Il trovatore, Excerpt (Deserto sulla terra)

Munich May 1939	Bavarian State Orchestra Zallinger Sung in German	78: Telefunken A 2963 LP: Telefunken HT 22/KT 11007 Some doubt has been cast about the authenticity of this recording, as no soprano and baritone soloists are named

RICHARD WAGNER (1813-1883)

Der fliegende Holländer, Excerpt (Willst jenes Tages)

Berlin	Städtische Oper	78: Telefunken E 3056
May 1939	Orchestra	LP: Telefunken HT 22/KT 11007
	Grüber	CD: Teldec 4509 955122

Der fliegende Holländer, Excerpt (Mit Gewitter und Sturm)

Berlin	Städtische Oper	78: Telefunken E 3056
December 1939	Orchestra	LP: Telefunken HT 22
	Grüber	CD: Teldec 4509 955122

Lohengrin

Cologne	Role of Lohengrin	LP: Rococo 1015
November 1951	Eipperle, H.Braun,	LP: Movimento musica 04.003
	Kronenberg,	CD: Myto MCD 93485
	Greindl, Ambrosius	Excerpts
	WDR Orchestra	LP: Acanta 40.23528
	and Chorus	CD: Acanta 43.268
	Kraus	CD: Bayer 200.029-200.030

Lohengrin, Excerpt (In fernem Land)

Baden-Baden	Südwestfunk	LP: Electrola E 83380/WCLP 781
April 1952	Orchestra	LP: EMI 1C 147 29142-29143M
	Ackermann	CD: EMI CDM 769 6822

Die Meistersinger von Nürnberg

London	Role of Stolzing	Unpublished radio broadcast
June-July	Grümmer,	Act 3 missing
1951	Shacklock, Dickie,	Excerpts
	Hotter/Kamann,	LP: Acanta DE 23.316-23.317/40.23528
	Weber, Kusche,	CD: Acanta 43.268
	G.Evans	
	Covent Garden	
	Orchestra & Chorus	
	Beecham	

Die Meistersinger von Nürnberg, Excerpt (Am stillen Herd)

Stuttgart	Württembergisches	78: DG LM 62 896
January 1953	Staatsorchester	45: DG NL 32 101
	Leitner	

Die Meistersinger von Nürnberg, Excerpt (Morgendlich leuchtend)

Stuttgart	Württembergisches	78: DG LM 62 896
January 1953	Staatsorchester	45: DG NL 32 101
	Leitner	LP: DG LPE 17 091/88 018/2721 212

CARL MARIA VON WEBER (1786-1826)

Der Freischütz, Querschnitt

Berlin	Koegel, Spletter,	78: Telefunken E 1943
1936	Nissen	
	Städtische Oper	
	Chorus	
	BPO	
	Schmidt-Isserstedt	

Der Freischütz, Excerpt (Nein, nicht länger trage ich die Qualen!)

Berlin	Städtische Oper	78: Telefunken E 2287
September 1937	Orchestra	LP: Telefunken HT 29/TW 30054/AJ642.232
	Schüler	CD: Teldec 4509 955122
Berlin	Städtische Oper	78: Electrola DA 5514
March 1952	Orchestra	LP: Electrola E 60006/E 83380/WCLP 781
	Rother	LP: EMI 1C 147 29142-29143M/EX769 7411
		CD: EMI CDM 769 6822/CHS 769 7412
Baden-Baden	Südwestfunk	LP: Acanta DE 23.316-23.317/40.23528
April 1952	Orchestra	CD: Acanta 43.268
	Ackermann	

Komponisten-Porträt Carl Maria von Weber

Berlin	Paetzold, Seegers	78: Telefunken E 1792
January 1935	Favres Choir	
	BPO	
	Schröder	

RICHARD WETZ (1875-1935)

Lieder: Die Liebe; Die Nachtigall; Wiegenlied

Berlin February 1945	Raucheisen	Unpublished radio broadcast

HUGO WOLF (1860-1903)

An den Schlaf (Schlaf, süsser Schlaf!)

Berlin November 1944	Raucheisen	LP: Acanta 40.23580 CD: Berlin Classics BC 21672

Frohe Botschaft (Hielt die allerschönste Herrin)

Berlin 1943-1944	Raucheisen	LP: Acanta 40.23581

Gesang Weylas/Mörike-Lieder (Du bist Orplid, mein Land!)

Hamburg 1952	Beckmann	Unpublished radio broadcast

Heimweh/Eichendorff-Lieder (Wer in die Fremde will wandern)

Berlin February 1945	Städtische Oper Orchestra Steinkopf	Unpublished radio broadcast
Cologne October 1948	Weissenborn	Unpublished radio broadcast

Heimweh/Mörike-Lieder (Anders wird die Welt mit jedem Schritt)

Berlin November 1944	Raucheisen	LP: Acanta 40.23580 CD: Berlin Classics BC 21672

Wolf Lieder/continued

Liebchen, wo bist du? (Zaub'rer bin ich, doch was frommt es?)

Berlin   Raucheisen   LP: Acanta 40.23581
November 1944

Liebesfrühling (Wie oft schon ward es Frühling wieder)

Berlin   Raucheisen   LP: Rococo 1015
1943-1944   LP: Acanta 40.23581

Lied des transferierten Zettels (Die Schwalbe, die den Sommer bringt)

Berlin   Raucheisen   LP: Acanta 40.23581
1943-1944

Der Musikant/Eichendorff-Lieder (Wandern lieb' ich für mein Leben)

Berlin   Raucheisen   45: DG EPL 30 524
January 1943   LP: DG 88 018
                                      LP: Melodiya M10 41895-41896
                                      LP: Acanta 40.23580
                                      CD: Berlin Classics BC 21672

Nachtgruss (In dem Himmel ruht die Erde)

Berlin   Raucheisen   LP: Rococo 1015
1943-1944   LP: Acanta 40.23581

Neue Liebe/Mörike-Lieder (Kann auch ein Mensch des andern auf der Erde)

Berlin   Raucheisen   LP: Acanta 40.23580
1943-1944

Nun wandre, Maria/Spanisches Liederbuch

Berlin   Raucheisen   45: DG EPL 30 522
1943-1944   LP: Acanta 40.23581
                                      CD: Berlin Classics BC 21672

Wolf Lieder/concluded

Schlafendes Jesuskind/Mörike-Lieder (Sohn der Jungfrau, Himmelskind!)

Berlin	Raucheisen	45: DG EPL 30 522
November 1944		LP: Acanta 40.23580
		CD: Berlin Classics BC 21672

Der Schwalben Heimkehr (Wenn die Schwalben heimwärts zieh'n)

Berlin	Raucheisen	LP: Acanta 40.23581
1943-1944		

Skolie (Reich' den Pokal mir schäumenden Weines voll!)

Berlin	Raucheisen	45: DG EPL 30 522
1943-1944		LP: Acanta 40.23581

Wanderers Nachtlied (Der du von dem Himmel bist)

Berlin	Raucheisen	45: DG EPL 30 522
November 1944		LP: Acanta 40.23581
		LP: Melodiya M10 41895-41896
		CD: Berlin Classics BC 21672

Weint nicht, ihr Aeuglein!/Spanisches Liederbuch

Berlin	Raucheisen	LP: Acanta 40.23581
1943-1944		

Wer tat deinem Füsslein weh?/Spanisches Liederbuch

Berlin	Raucheisen	LP: Acanta 40.23581
1943-1944		

Wohin mit der Freud'? (Ach, du klarblauer Himmel)

Berlin	Raucheisen	LP: Rococo 1015
1943-1944		LP: Acanta 40.23581

<u>Wolf Lieder sung by Anders also appear on Eterna LPs 820 442/822 610; 5 Wolf Lieder also recorded with Weissenborn in Cologne in October 1948 and tapes subsequently destroyed</u>

CARL ZELLER (1842-1898)

Der Kellermeister, Excerpt (Lass' dir Zeit!)

Baden-Baden July 1951	Südwestfunk Orchestra Burkhard	45: Electrola E 50578 LP: RCA VL 30319 CD: Acanta 43.812

Der Obersteiger, Excerpt (Sei nicht bös'!)

Berlin February 1936	Städtische Oper Orchestra & Chorus	78: Telefunken A 1925 LP: Telefunken HTP 515/NT 425/TS 3141
Baden-Baden July 1951	Südwestfunk Orchestra Burkhard	45: Electrola E 50578 LP: EMI 1C 147 29142-29143M CD: Acanta 43.812

Der Vogelhändler, Querschnitt

Cologne January 1953	Schlemm, Rothenberger, W.Hofmann, Himmelmann Sunshine-Quartett Cornel-Trio WDR Orchestra and Chorus Marszalek	78: Polydor LM 58 622 45: Polydor EPH 20 046 LP: Polydor LPHM 46 664/LPH 45 049 Excerpts 78: Polydor LM 48 927 45: Polydor EPH 20 121 LP: Polydor LPHM 46 757/2430 243 LP: DG 2721 212 CD: DG 447 6832

CARL ZIEHRER (1843-1922)

Die Landstreicher, Excerpt (Sei gepriesen, du lauschige Nacht!)

Cologne December 1953	WDR Orchestra Marszalek	78: Polydor LM 49 112 45: Polydor NH 22 121 LP: Polydor LPH 46 757/2430 243 LP: DG 2721 212 CD: DG 447 6832

PETER ANDERS SINGS POPULAR REPERTOIRE

Peter Anders im Land der Lieder, Melodienfolge

Cologne 1953	WDR Orchestra Marszalek	78: Polydor LM 58 617 45: Polydor EPH 20 035 <u>Excerpts</u> LP: Polydor LPHE 40 064/LPH 45 047

Du und Ich, Potpourri um Musik und Liebe

Berlin February 1934	Rautawaara Orchestra Bund	78: Telefunken A 1627

Alle Geigen singen: Nur Du!

Berlin February 1934	Orchestra Bund	78: Telefunken A 1626

Am Rhein bei Sankt Goar

Berlin October 1934	Orchestra Bund	78: Telefunken A 1685

Aus der Jugendzeit

Stuttgart February 1938	Reichssender Orchestra Görlich	Unpublished radio broadcast

Du bist nicht die Erste

Berlin	Orchestra	Telefunken unpublished

80   Anders

Endlos wie das Meer

Berlin	Orchestra	78: Telefunken A 1667
August 1934	Bund	45: Telefunken UX 5610

Die Frau der Frauen

Berlin	Orchestra	78: Telefunken A 1667
August 1934	Bund	45: Telefunken UX 5610
		LP: Telefunken NT 905

Für dich allein

Berlin	Orchestra	78: Telefunken A 1758
January 1935	Bund	45: Telefunken UX 5610

Granada

June 1953	Tanzorchester	78: Polydor LM 49 004
	Zacharias	45: Polydor NH 22 108
		LP: Polydor LPHE 40 064

Grossdeutschlands Dank

Date	Orchestra and	78: Telefunken T 6285
uncertain	Chorus	Special issue

Hörst du mein Lied?

Berlin	Orchestra	78: Telefunken A 1675
August 1934	Bund	

Ich schwör' auf Eine

Berlin	Orchestra	78: Telefunken A 1626
February 1934	Bund	

Liebesgeschichten, from the film Immer und ewig

Berlin	Orchestra	78: Electrola EG 7378
November 1949	Seidler-Winkler	45: Electrola E 20061
		LP: EMI 1C 147 29142-29143M

Mama mia, du vergiss' mich nicht!

Cologne	Tanz- und	78: Polydor LM 48 887/LM 49 004
December 1952	Unterhaltungs- orchester Luczkowsky	45: Polydor NH 22 108

Musik und Liebe, Excerpts (Mir hat ein Märchen heut' geträumt; Nun ist Frieden uns beschieden)

Berlin	Berger	78: Telefunken A 1467
August 1933	BPO J.Müller	LP: Telefunken HTP 515

Eine Nacht so blau (Blue Tango)

Cologne	Tanz- und	78: Polydor LM 48 887/LM 49 004
December 1952	Unterhaltungs- orchester Luczkowsky	45: Polydor NH 22 108

Nur im Traum darf ich glücklich sein

Berlin	Orchestra	78: Telefunken A 1685
October 1934	Bund	45: Telefunken UX 5610

O sole mio

Berlin	Städtische Oper	78: Telefunken A 2093
September 1936	Orchestra	LP: Telefunken HTP 515/DP 628.636

La paloma

Berlin	Städtische Oper	78: Telefunken A 2093
September 1936	Orchestra	LP: Telefunken HTP 515/DP 628.636

1000 rote Rosen blüh'n

Berlin   Orchestra   78: Telefunken A 1641
1934   Bund

Ueber die Prärie

Berlin   Orchestra   78: Telefunken A 1758
January 1935   Bund   LP: Telefunken HTP 515/NT 425/DP628.636

Von Wien durch die Welt, Potpourri

Berlin   Seegers   78: Telefunken E 1592
February 1934   Orchestra   LP: Telefunken HTP 517
                Bund

Unspecified items sung by Peter Anders also appear on the following LP labels:
Europa, Top Classic, Marcato and Melodiya (M10 47403 002)

Opposite page: 1945 performance of Rigoletto by Berlin Staatsoper with Anders, Berger and Burgwinkel, presumably given for the occupying Russian authorities; Streich sings small role of the Page

Немецкая государственная опера
в здании Адмиральспаласта
Фридрихштрассе 101/102

Новая инсценировка
„Риголетто"
опера в 4 картинах
Музыка Джюзеппе Верди
Текст Фр. М. Пиаве

Дирижер: Иоганнес Шюлер   Постановка: Вольф Фелькер
Декорации: Лотар Шенк фон Трапп

УЧАСТВУЮЩИЕ:

Герцог Мантуи	Петер Андерс
Риголетто, шут	Иосиф Бургвинкель
Джильда, его дочь	Эрна Бергер
Спарафучиле, разбойник	Иосиф Грейндль
Магдалена, его сестра	Карола Герлих
Джиованна, прислужница	Эльфрида Маргерр
Граф Монтероне	Яро Прохазка
Марулло, кавалер	Вальтер Штолль
Борза, придворный	Фридрих Бушман
Граф Чепрано	Отто Гопф
Графиня Чепрано	Елена Влашек
Служащий в замке	Вилли Поллов
Паж герцогини	Рита Штрейх

Придворные, пажи, геллебардиры

Костюмы: Курт Пальм
Техническая часть: Макс Гибнер

Перемена в составе исполнителей допустима

Антракт после 2-ой картины

Начало 16.30 часов   Конец 19 часов

Walther Ludwig
1902-1981

Discography compiled
by John Hunt

DANIEL AUBER (1782-1871)

Fra Diavolo, Excerpt (Pour toujours, disait-elle)

Munich July 1951	Munich PO Lehmann Sung in German	DG unpublished
Munich October 1951	Bavarian State Orchestra Lehmann Sung in German	78: DG LV 36 059 45: DG EPL 30 007

JOHANN SEBASTIAN BACH (1685-1750)

Cantata No 6 "Bleib bei uns, denn es will Abend werden", Excerpt (Es hat die Dunkelheit an vielen Orten/Jesu, lass uns auf dich sehen!)

Leipzig April 1933	Gewandhaus Orchestra Thomanerchor Straube	Unpublished radio broadcast

Cantata No 189 "Meine Seele rühmt und preist"

Munich 1951	Instrumentalists Lehmann	78: DG 2427-2428 LP: DG APM 14 028 LP: Decca (USA) DL 9619 Also published on 78s by Supraphon

Mass in B minor

Vienna June 1950	Schwarzkopf, Ferrier, Poell, Schöffler Wiener Singverein VSO Karajan	CD: Foyer 2CF-2022 CD: Hunt CDKAR 212 CD: Verona 27073-27074

Saint Matthew Passion

Berlin 1942	Evangelist and tenor arias Briem, Hammer, Nissen Kittel Choir BPO Kittel	78: Grammophon 67951-67968 CD: Philips Shinseido (Japan) SGR 6011-6013 Ich will bei meinem Jesu wachen 78: DG 68437
Vienna November 1948	Schwarzkopf, Höngen, Braun, Schmitt-Walter Wiener Singverein VPO Karajan	Soundtrack only for a film depicting the Passion story with paintings from the 15th-17th centuries; some spoken commentary is imposed over the music
Vienna June 1950	Seefried, Ferrier, Edelmann, Wiener, Schöffler, Berry Wiener Singverein VSO Karajan	LP: Foyer FO 1046 CD: Foyer 3CF-2013 CD: Hunt CDKAR 211 CD: Verona 27070-27072

Saint Matthew Passion, Excerpt (Ich will bei meinem Jesu wachen)

Munich February 1951	Bavarian Radio Orchestra & Chorus Jochum	Unpublished radio broadcast

LUDWIG VAN BEETHOVEN (1770-1827)

Symphony No 9 "Choral"

London May 1937	Berger, Pitzinger, Watzke BPO Philharmonic Choir of London Furtwängler	LP: EMI ED 27 01231 LP: Toshiba WF 60073-60074 CD: Toshiba TOCE 6057 CD: Music and Arts CD 818 <u>Music and Arts incorrectly describes chorus as Bruno Kittel Choir</u>
Hamburg 1938	Fahrni, Hammer, Watzke Philharmonisches Staatsorchester and Chorus Jochum	78: Telefunken SK 2615-2623
Munich 1953	Ebers, Pitzinger, Frantz Bavarian Radio Orchestra & Chorus Jochum	78: DG LVM 72 306-72 310 LP: DG LP 16 070 & LPM 18 070/ LPEM 19293-19299 <u>Last movement</u> LP: DG LPEM 19 074
Hamburg 1956-1957	G.Weber, Boese, Watzke Hamburg Pro Musica Orchestra & Chorus Walther	LP: MEL 5004-5005 LP: World Records T 56-T 57

Fidelio, Excerpt (Er sterbe! Doch er soll erst wissen!)

Berlin 1932	Gottlieb, Domgraf-Fassbänder, Grossmann Staatskapelle Zweig	78: Electrola DB 4417 78: Victor 11826 LP: Preiser LV 120 LP: Historia H 644

Adelaide (Einsam wandelt dein Freund)

July 1958	Bohle	45: DG EPL 30 517/SEP 121 016

Ludwig

An die ferne Geliebte, Song cycle

Berlin 1956	Bohle	45: Eterna 520 095

Die Klage (Turteltaube, du klagest so laut!)

Berlin 1942-1944	Raucheisen	LP: Acanta 40.23535

Der Kuss (Ich war bei Chloen ganz allein)

Berlin January 1937	Leitner	78: Electrola EG 4016/GX 254 LP: Historia H 712-713
Berlin 1942-1944	Raucheisen	LP: Acanta 40.23535
July 1958	Bohle	45: DG EPL 30 517/SEP 121 016

Mit einem gemalten Band (Kleine Blumen, kleine Blätter)

Berlin 1942-1944	Raucheisen	LP: Acanta 40.23535
July 1958	Bohle	45: DG EPL 30 517/SEP 121 016

Neue Liebe, neues Leben (Herz, mein Herz, was soll das geben?)

Berlin 1942-1944	Raucheisen	LP: Acanta 40.23535
July 1958	Bohle	45: DG EPL 30 517/SEP 121 016

Zärtliche Liebe (Ich liebe dich, sowie du mich)

Berlin January 1937	Leitner	78: Electrola EG 4016/GX 254
July 1958	Bohle	45: DG EPL 30 517/SEP 121 016

CESARE BIXIO (1898-1978)

Parlami d'amore

Berlin May 1934	Orchestra Dobrindt Sung in German	78: Electrola EG 3060

GEORGES BIZET (1838-1875)

Carmen, Excerpt (Parle-moi de ma mère!)

Berlin 1937	Perras Staatskapelle Seidler-Winkler Sung in German	78: Electrola EH 1036 LP: Preiser LV 232/LV 1312 CD: Preiser 89088
Berlin 1944	L.Hoffman Berlin RO Rother Sung in German	Unpublished radio broadcast
Munich 1951	Trötschel Bavarian State Orchestra Leitner Sung in German	78: DG LV 36 003 45: DG NL 32 203

Les pêcheurs de perles, Excerpt (Je crois entendre encore)

Berlin 1944	Berlin RO Rother Sung in German	LP: BASF 22 21492-5
Berlin 1956	Berlin RO Stein Sung in German	LP: Eterna 821 075/822 604-822 605

92 Ludwig

Les pêcheurs de perles, Excerpt (Au fond du temple saint)

Berlin 1946	Schmitt-Walter Berlin RO Dobrindt Sung in German	LP: BASF 22 21492-5/22 21498-3/BB 23.119
Berlin 1956	Schmitt-Walter Berlin RO Stein Sung in German	Unpublished radio broadcast

FRANCOIS BOIELDIEU (1775-1834)

La dame blanche

Stuttgart November 1937	Role of George Formacher, Madlen-Madsen, Waldenau, Hann, Buchta, A.Welitsch Reichssender Orchestra & Chorus Görlich Sung in German	Unpublished radio broadcast

La dame blanche, Excerpt (Viens, gentille Dame!)

Berlin 1943	Berlin RO Rother Sung in German	LP: BASF 22 21492-5 LP: Eterna 821075/822 671-822 672 LP: Acanta 40.23544 LP: Historia H 712-713
Stuttgart October 1952	Württembergisches Staatsorchester Leitner Sung in German	78: DG LV 36 059 45: DG EPL 32 202

JOHANNES BRAHMS (1833-1897)

Auf dem Kirchhofe (Der Tag ging regenschwer und sturmbewegt)

Munich   Altmann   Unpublished radio broadcast
1956

Botschaft (Wehe, Lüftchen, lind und lieblich)

Munich   Altmann   Unpublished radio broadcast
1956

Dämm'rung senkte sich von oben

Munich   Altmann   Unpublished radio broadcast
1956

Feldeinsamkeit (Ich ruhe still im hohen grünen Gras)

Munich   Altmann   Unpublished radio broadcast
1956

Heimweh II (O wüsst' ich doch den Weg zurück)

Berlin   Raucheisen   LP: Acanta 40.23524
1942

Munich   Altmann   Unpublished radio broadcast
1956

Junge Lieder I (Meine Liebe ist grün)

Munich   Altmann   Unpublished radio broadcast
1956

Brahms Lieder/continued

Liebeslieder-Walzer

Berlin	Berger, Pitzinger,	LP: Quadriga-Ton 703-704
1957	Wenke	CD: FNAC Music 642.313
	Falbe, Scherzer	

Liebliches Kind

Bremen	Bohle	Unpublished radio broadcast
1953		
Munich	Altmann	Unpublished radio broadcast
1956		

Mein Mädel hat einen Rosenmund/Deutsche Volkslieder

Berlin	Berlin String	78: Electrola EG 3329
January 1935	Quartet	
	Seidler-Winkler, piano	

Minnelied (Holder klingt der Vogelsang)

Bremen	Bohle	Unpublished radio broadcast
1953		

Neue Liebeslieder-Walzer

Berlin	Berger, Pitzinger,	LP: Quadriga-Ton 703-704
1957	Wenke	CD: FNAC Music 642.313
	Falbe, Scherzer	

O liebliche Wangen, ihr macht mich Verlangen!

Munich	Altmann	Unpublished radio broadcast
1956		

Brahms Lieder/continued

Salamander (Es sass ein Salamander)

Bremen 1953	Bohle	Unpublished radio broadcast

Die Schnur, die Perl' an Perle

Berlin 1942	Raucheisen	LP: Acanta 40.23524
Bremen 1953	Bohle	Unpublished radio broadcast

Ständchen (Der Mond steht über dem Berge)

Berlin 1942	Raucheisen	LP: Acanta 40.23524/DE 23125-23126
Berlin 1944	Raucheisen	Unpublished radio broadcast

Wie bist du, meine Königin?

Bremen 1953	Bohle	Unpublished radio broadcast

Wir wandelten, wir zwei zusammen

Bremen 1953	Bohle	Unpublished radio broadcast
Munich 1956	Altmann	Unpublished radio broadcast

8 Zigeunerlieder

Berlin 1939	Leitner	78: Grammophon 47310-47311
Stuttgart March 1951	Giesen	Unpublished radio broadcast
Munich 1956	Altmann	Unpublished radio broadcast

96 Ludwig

PETER CORNELIUS (1824-1874)

Der Barbier von Bagdad

Berlin October 1934	<u>Role of Nureddin</u> Nettesheim, Baum, Kiefer, Bohnen Funkorchester and Chorus Rosbaud	Unpublished radio broadcast
Stuttgart April 1939	Eipperle, Waldenau, Hann, A.Welitsch Reichssender Orchestra & Chorus Leonhardt	Unpublished radio broadcast

Der Barbier von Bagdad, Excerpt (Vor deinem Fenster die Blumen)

Frankfurt 1950	Hessischer Rundfunk Orchestra Schröder	Unpublished radio broadcast

Der Barbier von Bagdad, Excerpt (Mein Sohn, sei Allahs Frieden!)

Frankfurt August 1937	Andresen Frankfurt RO Rosbaud	Unpublished radio broadcast
Stuttgart November 1937	Hann Reichssender Orchestra Görlich	Unpublished radio broadcast
Berlin 1943	Hann Berlin RO Rother	LP: BASF 22 21486-9

Dein Bildnis

Berlin   Raucheisen   LP: Acanta 40.23503
1942-1944

In der Ferne

Berlin   Raucheisen   LP: Acanta 40.23503
1942-1944

Sei mein

Berlin   Raucheisen   LP: Acanta 40.23503
1942-1944

Wie lieb ich dich hab'

Berlin   Raucheisen   LP: Acanta 40.23503
1942-1944

98 Ludwig

GAETONO DONIZETTI (1797-1848)

L'elisir d'amore, Extracts

Berlin June 1942	<u>Role of Nemorino</u> Beilke, Wocke, Windisch Städtische Oper Orchestra & Chorus Lutze <u>Sung in German</u>	LP: Melodiya M10 46955 001 LP: BASF 22 21492-5

L'elisir d'amore, Excerpt (Una furtiva lagrima)

Berlin 1944	Berlin RO Steinkopf <u>Sung in German</u>	Unpublished radio broadcast
Frankfurt 1951	Hessischer Rundfunk Orchestra Schröder <u>Sung in German</u>	Unpublished radio broadcast
Berlin 1956	Berlin RO Stein <u>Sung in German</u>	45: Eterna 520 117 LP: Eterna 821 075

L'elisir d'amore, Excerpt (Una parola, Adina!)

Berlin 1937	Beilke Berlin RO <u>Sung in German</u>	LP: Historia H 683-684

L'elisir d'amore, Excerpt (Venti scudi!)

Berlin 1946	Schmitt-Walter Berlin RO Dobrindt <u>Sung in German</u>	LP: BASF 22 21498-3
Berlin 1956	Schmitt-Walter Berlin RO Stein <u>Sung in German</u>	45: Eterna 520 117 LP: Eterna 821 075

ANTONIN DVORAK (1841-1904)

The Jacobin, Excerpt (How must I suffer?)

Leipzig December 1956	Leipzig RO Pflüger Sung in German	Unpublished radio broadcast

7 Gypsy Melodies

Berlin 1943	Raucheisen Sung in German	LP: Melodiya M10 47335 000/M10 47335 006
Munich 1948	Altmann Sung in German	Unpublished radio broadcast
Stuttgart March 1949	Giesen Sung in German	Unpublished radio broadcast

2 Duets: Destined; The Parting

Berlin 1943	Scheppan Raucheisen Sung in German	LP: Melodiya M10 47335 000/M10 47335 006

ROBERT ERNST

Kalendarium

Berlin October 1942	Raucheisen	Unpublished radio broadcast

PHILIPP EULENBURG (1847-1921)

5 Rosenlieder: Monatsrose; Wilde Rose; Rankende Rose; Seerose; Weisse und rote Rose

October 1957	Bohle	45: DG EPL 30 296

100 Ludwig

LEO FALL (1873-1925)

Die Kaiserin, Querschnitt

Berlin December 1933	Frind Orchestra Etlinger	78: Electrola EH 859 LP: PR 10 CD: Centaur CRC 2116

FRIEDRICH FLOTOW (1812-1883)

Alessandro Stradella, Excerpt (Jungfrau Maria)

Berlin September 1932	Städtische Oper Orchestra Ladwig	78: Electrola EH 810 LP: Electrola E 83385/WCLP 791 LP: Preiser LV 232 CD: Preiser 89088
Berlin July 1937	Reichssender and Deutschlandsender Orchestras Steiner	Unpublished radio broadcast
Berlin December 1937	Kurzwellensender Orchestra Wicke	Unpublished radio broadcast
Berlin 1944	Städtische Oper Orchestra Rother	LP: BASF 22 21492-5 LP: Eterna 821 075 LP: Melodiya M10 46863 008
Frankfurt 1950-1951	Hessischer Rundfunk Orchestra Schröder	Unpublished radio broadcast

Martha, Excerpt (Ach so fromm)

Königsberg February 1940	Reichssender Orchestra Wöller	Unpublished radio broadcast
Stuttgart April 1951	Württembergisches Staatsorchester Leitner	78: DG L 62 878 45: DG EPL 30 293 LP: DG LPE 17007 LP: Eterna 720 084/821 075

Martha, Excerpt (Seit früher Kindheit Tagen)

Berlin 1937	Strienz Orchestra Seidler-Winkler	78: Electrola EH 1083 LP: Electrola E 83385/WCLP 791

Martha, Excerpt (Mag der Himmel euch vergeben!)

Stuttgart April 1951	Wissmann Württembergisches Staatsorchester Leitner	78: DG L 62 878 45: DG EPL 30 293 LP: DG LPE 17 007 LP: Eterna 720 084

Martha, Excerpt (Nancy! Julia!)

Berlin October 1941	Reichelt Orchestra Rother	Unpublished radio broadcast

ROBERT FRANZ (1815-1892)

3 Lieder: Waldfahrt; Abends; Willkommen, mein Held!

Bremen 1953	Bohle	Unpublished radio broadcast

102 Ludwig

CHRISTOPH WILLIBALD GLUCK (1714-1787)

Paride ed Elena, Excerpt (O del mio dolce ardor!)

Berlin November 1942	Raucheisen	LP: Melodiya M10 46863 008

PAUL GRAENER (1872-1944)

Friedemann Bach, Excerpt (Kein Hälmlein wächst auf Erden)

Berlin September 1932	Städtische Oper Orchestra Ladwig	78: Electrola EG 2644 LP: Electrola E 83385/WCLP 791 LP: Historia H 712-713 LP: Preiser LV 232 CD: Preiser 89088

Friedemann Bach, Excerpt (Preis dir und Dank!)

Berlin September 1932	Städtische Oper Orchestra Ladwig	78: Electrola EG 2644 LP: Historia H 712-713 LP: Preiser LV 232 CD: Preiser 89088

Hanneles Himmelfahrt

Berlin March 1937	Roles of Gottwald and Fremder Eipperle, Arndt-Ober, De Vogt, Byler Reichssender Orchestra & Chorus Graener	Unpublished radio broadcast

Lieder: Der Kuckuck; Der König

Berlin 1935	Leitner	78: Electrola EG 3366 CD: Preiser 89088

ALEXANDER GRETCHANINOV (1864-1956)

Cradle Song

Berlin	Leitner	78: Grammophon 62824
1941	Sung in German	

EDVARD GRIEG (1843-1907)

Eros

Berlin	Leitner	78: Electrola EG 3242
November 1934	Sung in German	

Lys nat

Berlin	Raucheisen	LP: Melodiya M10 46863 008
1944	Sung in German	

FRANZ XAVER GRUBER (1787-1863)

Stille Nacht, heilige Nacht

Berlin	Instrumentalists	78: Grammophon 47257
1938		78: Supraphon C 191140

GEORGE FRIDERIC HANDEL (1685-1759)

Ode to Saint Cecilia

Berlin	L.Hoffman	LP: Urania UR 7023
Date uncertain	Lamy Choir	
	Berlin RO	
	Rother	
	Sung in German	

FRANZ JOSEF HAYDN (1732-1809)

Die Jahreszeiten

Berlin
January 1952
	Trötschel, Greindl
	St Hedwig's and
	RIAS Choirs
	Berlin RO
	Fricsay
		LP: DG LPM 18 025-18 028/
		    LPM 18 486-18 488/2701 010/2721 170
		LP: Decca (USA) DX 123
		Excerpts
		78: DG 36076/72406
		LP: DG LPE 17 225/LPEM 19 307/
		    LPEM 19 364/136 326

Die Schöpfung

Munich May 1951	Seefried, Hotter Bavarian Radio Orchestra & Chorus Jochum	LP: Melodram MEL 208 LP: Movimento musica 02.021

ARTHUR HONEGGER (1892-1955)

Le roi David

Berlin September- October 1952	Trötschel, L.Fischer, S.Schneider Berlin Radio Orchestra & Chorus St Hedwig's Choir Fricsay Sung in German	Unpublished radio broadcast

EMMERICH KALMAN (1882-1953)

Die Czardasfürstin, Querschnitt

Berlin November 1934	Frind 5 Parodisters Orchestra Schönbaumsfeld	78: Electrola EH 902 LP: PR 10

Gräfin Maritza, Excerpt (Grüss' mir mein Wien)

Munich September 1951	Bavaria SO Schmidt-Boelcke	78: Polydor 48578

HEINRICH KAMINSKI (1886-1946)

Jürg Jenatsch, Extract

Berlin December 1932	Unnamed soloists, orchestra and conductor	Unpublished radio broadcast

WILHELM KIENZL (1857-1941)

Der Evangelimann, Excerpt (Selig sind, die Verfolgung leiden)

Berlin 1940	Staatskapelle and Chorus Steeger	78: Grammophon 15477 LP: Historia H 712-713 CD: Preiser 89088

Der Kuhreigen, Excerpt (Zu Strassburg auf der Schanz)

Berlin September 1940	Deutschlandsender Orchestra & Chorus Rother	Unpublished radio broadcast
Berlin 1940	Staatskapelle and Chorus Steeger	78: Grammophon 15477 LP: Historia H 712-713 CD: Preiser 89088

ARMIN KNAB (1881-1951)

Inschrift; Arie zu einer kleinen Nachtmusik; Sommer

Berlin November 1938	Vulté	Unpublished radio broadcast

106 Ludwig

CONRADIN KREUTZER (1780-1849)

Das Nachtlager von Granada

Berlin March 1934	Role of Gomez Jungkurth, Domgraf-Fassbaender Funkorchester and Chorus Steiner	Unpublished radio broadcast

Das Nachtlager von Granada, Excerpt (Trenne nicht das Band der Liebe)

Berlin February 1934	E.Friedrich, Hüsch Städtische Oper Orchestra Zaun	Electrola unpublished
Berlin March 1934	E.Friedrich, Hüsch Städtische Oper Orchestra Zaun	78: Electrola EH 864/FKX 174 LP: Preiser LV 76

FRANZ LEHAR (1870-1948)

Die lustige Witwe, Querschnitt

Munich 1951	Role of Danilo Trötschel, Bak, W.Hofmann Munich PO and Chorus Nick	78: Polydor 58601 LP: Polydor LPH 45020/LPHM 46510 LP: Decca (USA) DL 4001 LP: DG 478 107

Paganini, Querschnitt

Berlin 1937	Role of Paganini Frind Orchestra & Chorus Seidler-Winkler	78: Electrola EH 1046 LP: PR 10

Paganini, Excerpt (Niemand liebt dich so wie ich)

Berlin March 1936	Jungkurth Staatskapelle Seidler-Winkler	78: Electrola EG 3641
Berlin 1940	Claus Staatskapelle Steeger	78: Grammophon 15338

Der Rastelbinder, Excerpt (Wenn zwei sich lieben)

Berlin March 1936	Staatskapelle Seidler-Winkler	78: Electrola EG 3633 LP: Electrola E 83343 LP: Eterna (USA) 735 LP: EMI 1C 137 46347-46348M

Der Zarewitsch, Querschnitt

Berlin March 1936	Jungkurth Staatskapelle Seidler-Winkler	78: Electrola EG 3641

FRANZ LISZT (1811-1886)

Es muss ein Wunderbares sein

Bremen 1959	Bohle	Unpublished radio broadcast

Im Rhein, am schönen Strome

Stuttgart Date uncertain	Giesen	Unpublished radio broadcast
Bremen 1959	Bohle	Unpublished radio broadcast

108 Ludwig

Undine, Excerpt (Vater, Mutter, Schwestern, Brüder!)

Stuttgart October 1952	Württembergisches Staatsorchester Leitner	DG unpublished
Munich December 1953	Bamberg SO Reinshagen	45: DG EPL 32 075 LP: DG LPEM 19 010
Leipzig Date uncertain	Leipzig RO Masur	Unpublished radio broadcast

Undine, Excerpt (Was seh' ich?/Ihr seid glücklich wieder da!)

Munich December 1953	Blankenheim Bamberg SO Reinshagen	45: DG EPL 30 277 LP: DG LPEM 19 010

Der Wildschütz (Kann es im Erdenleben)

Berlin 1932	E.Friedrich, Klose, Domgraf-Fassbaender Staatskapelle Lutze	78: Electrola EH 850/FKX 177 LP: Electrola E 83385/WCLP 791 LP: Preiser LV 120

Lortzing-Meisterporträt

Berlin January 1935	Frind, Hüsch, Strienz Orchestra H.-U. Müller	78: Electrola EH 907

MARK LOTHAR (1902-1985)

Das kalte Herz

Berlin March 1935	<u>Role of Peter</u> Tegethoff, Jungkurth, Hellmer, Grossmann Deutschlandsender Orchestra & Chorus Lothar	Unpublished radio broadcast

CARL LOEWE (1796-1869)

Die Uhr

Berlin June 1934	Leitner	78: Electrola EH 879 LP: Preiser LV 200

Tom der Reimer

Berlin June 1934	Leitner	78: Electrola EH 879

ALBERT LORTZING (1801-1851)

Zar und Zimmermann

Stuttgart
November 1952
	Role of
	Chateauneuf
	Junker-Giesen,
	T.Anders, Pfeifle,
	Günter, Neidlinger
	Württembergisches
	Staatsorchester
	and Chorus
	Leitner
		LP: DG LPM 18 060-18 062/
		    LPM 18 126-18 128
		LP: Decca (USA) DX 129
		Excerpts
		78: DG LV 36 061
		45: DG EPL 32 075
		LP: DG LPE 17107/LPEM 19313/
		    LPEM 19365

Zar und Zimmermann, Excerpt (Leb wohl, mein flandrisch Mädchen!)

Berlin November 1941	Rudolph Städtische Oper Orchestra & Chorus Steinkopf	Unpublished radio broadcast

Ludwig

GUSTAV MAHLER (1860-1911)

Lieder eines fahrenden Gesellen

Munich   Altmann   Unpublished radio broadcast
1947

JOHANN PAUL MARTINI (1741-1816)

Plaisir d'amour

Leipzig   Leipzig RO   Unpublished radio broadcast
December 1956   Fricke

JULES MASSENET (1842-1912)

Werther, Excerpt (Pourquoi me réveiller?)

Leipzig   Leipzig RO   Unpublished radio broadcast
January 1957   Masur
                Sung in German

CARL MILLOECKER (1842-1899)

Der Bettelstudent, Excerpt (Ich setz' den Fall)

Berlin September 1934	Jungkurth Staatskapelle and Chorus Schönbaumsfeld	78: Electrola EH 893/FKX 84 LP: Historia H 712-713

Gasparone, Excerpt (Dunkelrote Rosen)

Berlin March 1936	Staatskapelle Seidler-Winkler	78: Electrola EH 3633
Berlin 1940	Staatskapelle	78: Grammophon 15382
Berlin 1940	Orchestra	Unpublished radio broadcast

112 Ludwig

WOLFGANG AMADEUS MOZART (1756-1791)

Così fan tutte, Excerpt (Un aura amorosa)

Berlin January 1936	Staatskapelle Seidler-Winkler <u>Sung in German</u>	78: Electrola EH 957 LP: Preiser LV 232 CD: Preiser 89088
Berlin October 1944	Berlin RO Rother <u>Sung in German</u>	Unpublished radio broadcast
Vienna November 1948	VPO Prohaska <u>Sung in German</u>	Columbia unpublished

Don Giovanni, Excerpt (Dalla sua pace)

Berlin December 1933	Orchestra Benda <u>Sung in German</u>	78: Electrola EH 837/FKX 180 LP: Electrola E 83385/WCLP 791 LP: Historia H 712-713 LP: Preiser LV 232 CD: Preiser 89088 <u>Historia incorrectly dated 1944</u>
Vienna November 1948	VPO Prohaska <u>Sung in German</u>	78: Columbia LX 1260
Stuttgart October 1952	Württembergisches Staatsorchester Leitner <u>Sung in German</u>	78: DG 72305 45: DG EPL 30 033 LP: Decca (USA) DL 4073
Stuttgart October 1952	Württembergisches Staatsorchester Leitner	LP: DG LPM 18 558-18 559
Leipzig November 1956	Leipzig RO Stein <u>Sung in German</u>	Unpublished radio broadcast

Don Giovanni, Excerpt (Il mio tesoro)

Vienna November 1948	VPO Prohaska Sung in German	78: Columbia LX 1260
Stuttgart 1948	SDR Orchestra Müller-Kray Sung in German	Unpublished radio broadcast
Stuttgart October 1952	Württembergisches Staatsorchester Leitner Sung in German	78: DG 72305 45: DG EPL 30 033 LP: DG LPE 17 014 LP: Decca (USA) DL 4073
Stuttgart October 1952	Württembergisches Staatsorchester Leitner	DG unpublished

Die Entführung aus dem Serail

Stuttgart May 1938	Role of Belmonte Berger, Beilke, Buchta, S.Nilsson Reichssender Orchestra & Chorus Böhm	Unpublished radio broadcast
Hamburg March 1946	Berger, Wulff, Pfeifle, T.Hermann NDR Orchestra and Chorus Schmidt-Isserstedt	Unpublished radio broadcast Excerpts LP: Ed Smith EJS 574 LP: Allegro ALL 3090 Allegro edition uses pseudonyms for the performers
Vienna June 1950	Lipp, Loose, Klein, Koreh Vienna Opera Chorus VPO Krips	78: Decca (Switzerland) K28341-28353 LP: Decca LXT 2536-2538 LP: London (USA) LLPA 3/RS 63015 LP: Decca ECM 730-731/411 6741 CD: Decca 443 5302 Excerpts 78: Decca K 23267 LP: Decca LXT 2635 LP: Telefunken BLK 20522/VD 625 LP: DG 429 8401

Ludwig

Die Entführung aus dem Serail, Excerpt (O wie ängstlich!)

Berlin January 1936	Staatskapelle Seidler-Winkler	78: Electrola EH 957 LP: Preiser LV 232
Munich 1948	Bavarian State Orchestra Leitner	78: DG 57342/68295
Vienna November 1949	VPO Loibner	LP: EMI RLS 764/1C 137 43187-43189
Munich August 1951	Bavarian State Orchestra Leitner	78: DG 68469

Die Entführung aus dem Serail, Excerpt (Wenn der Freude Tränen fliessen)

Berlin December 1933	Orchestra Benda	78: Electrola EH 837/FKX 180 LP: Electrola E 83385 LP: Preiser LV 232 CD: Preiser 89088
Berlin 1945	Berlin RO Rother	LP: BASF 22 21492-5
Vienna November 1949	VPO Loibner	LP: EMI RLS 764/1C 137 43187-43189
Stuttgart April 1951	Württembergisches Staatsorchester Leitner	78: DG 68469 45: DG EPL 30 033

Die Entführung aus dem Serail, Excerpt (Vivat Bacchus!)

Berlin 1937	Strienz Orchestra Seidler-Winkler	78: Electrola EG 6347/JK 2378 LP: Electrola E 83385/WCLP 791 LP: Eterna (USA) 742 LP: Preiser LV 1357

La finta giardiniero, Excerpt (Tu mi lasci?)

Berlin 1937	Reichelt Orchestra Seidler-Winkler Sung in German	78: Electrola EG 3988 LP: Electrola E 83385/WCLP 791 LP: Historia H 712-713

Idomeneo, Excerpt (Il padre adorato)

Berlin 1943	Berlin RO Rother <u>Sung in German</u>	Unpublished radio broadcast

Per pietà non ricercate, Concert aria

Stuttgart 1948	SDR Orchestra Müller-Kray	Unpublished radio broadcast
Leipzig January 1957	Leipzig RO Masur	Unpublished radio broadcast

Requiem

Berlin 1941	Briem, Freimuth, Frissen Kittel Choir BPO Kittel	78: Grammophon 67731-67739 CD: Philips Shinseido (Japan) SGR 6011-6013

Vienna
June 1950
	Pech, Breitschopf,
	Pröglhöf
	Hofmusikkapelle
	and Chorus
	Krips
		78: Decca X 53028-53034/AX 366-372
		78: Decca (Switzerland) K28327-28333
		LP: Decca LX 3030-3031/LXT 2013/
		   ACL 39/ECS 715/411 6821
		LP: Telefunken ND 377
		LP: London (USA) LPS 230-231/
		   B 19077/R 23246

Die Verschweigung

Berlin June 1943	Raucheisen	LP: Melodiya M10 46863 008

116 Ludwig

Die Zauberflöte

Berlin April 1936	<u>Role of Tamino</u> Callam, Armhold, Rudolph, Wocke, Manowarda Deutschlandsender Orchestra & Chorus Stange	Unpublished radio broadcast
Stuttgart December 1937	Eipperle, Piltti, Preisig, Hann, Schmitt-Walter, Manowarda Reichsender Orchestra & Chorus Keilberth	Unpublished radio broadcast
Berlin December 1937	Lemnitz, Berger, Rudolph, Alsen, Hezel, Domgraf-Fassbänder Favre Choir Reichsender Orchestra Steiner	Unpublished radio broadcast <u>Excerpts</u> LP: BASF 22 21490-3
Salzburg July 1949	Seefried, Lipp, Oravez, Greindl, Schmitt-Walter, Schöffler Vienna Opera Chorus VPO Furtwängler	LP: Ed Smith EJS 572 LP: Hope Records HOPE 208 LP: Discocorp IGI 337 LP: Columbia (Japan) OZ 7572-7574 LP: Cetra (Japan) GT 7093-7095 CD: Arlecchino ARL 78-80 CD: Music and Arts CD 882 <u>Excerpts</u> LP: Melodram MEL 084 CD: Di Stefano GDS 1206
Stuttgart December 1949	Wissmann, Jäger, Schmitt-Walter, Rohr SDR Orchestra and Chorus Müller-Kray	Unpublished radio broadcast

Die Zauberflöte, Excerpt (Dies Bildnis ist bezaubernd schön)

Berlin 1943	Berlin RO Rother	LP: BASF 22 21492-5 CD: Minerva MNA 21
Vienna February 1949	VPO Ackermann	LP: EMI EX 769 7411 CD: EMI CHS 769 7412
Vienna November 1949	VPO Loibner	Columbia unpublished

Die Zauberflöte, Excerpt (Wie stark ist nicht dein Zauberton)

Berlin January 1937	Orchestra Seidler-Winkler	78: Electrola EH 1020 LP: EMI 1C 137 46347-46348M LP: Preiser LV 232 CD: Preiser 89088
Leipzig November 1956	Leipzig RO	Unpublished radio broadcast

OTTO NICOLAI (1810-1849)

Die lustigen Weiber von Windsor

Berlin May 1943	Role of Fenton Beilke, Schilp, L.Hoffman, Hann, Strienz, Florian Städtische Oper Chorus Berlin RO Rother	LP: Urania UR 5214/US 5214 LP: BASF 22 21492-5 Excerpts LP: Saga FID 2137 LP: BASF 05.21549-0

Die lustigen Weiber von Windsor, Unspecified exctracts

Berlin 1943	L.Hoffman, Hann Berlin RO Steinkopf	Unpublished radio broadcast

118 Ludwig

Die lustigen Weiber von Windsor, Excerpt (Horch, die Lerche singt im Hain)

Berlin January 1937	Orchestra Seidler-Winkler	78: Electrola EH 1020 LP: Electrola E 83385/WCLP 791 LP: Marcato 343.996 LP: Preiser LV 232 CD: Preiser 89088
Stuttgart July 1951	Württembergisches Staatsorchester Leitner	78: DG LV 36 009 45: DG EPL 30 293 LP: DG LPEM 19 049/89 648 LP: Eterna 821.075

JACQUES OFFENBACH (1819-1880)

Les contes d'Hoffmann, Excerpt (Il était une fois à la cour d'Eisenach)

Stuttgart April 1951	Württembergisches Staatsorchester Leitner Sung in German	78: DG LV 36 001 45: DG EPL 30 554 LP: DG LPE 17 049

Les contes d'Hoffmann, Excerpt (C'est un chanson d'amour)

Stuttgart April 1951	Wissmann Württembergisches Staatsorchester Leitner Sung in German	DG unpublished
Berlin 1951	Grümmer Berlin RO Lehmann Sung in German	LP: Melodram MEL 083

GIOVANNI PAISIELLO (1740-1816)

La molinara, Excerpt (All my joy is gone)

Date uncertain	Giebel Bohle Sung in German	Unpublished radio broadcast

I zingari in fiera, Excerpt (Chi vuoi la zingarella)

Berlin October 1942	Raucheisen	LP: Melodiya M10 46863 008
Leipzig December 1956	Leipzig RO Fricke	Unpublished radio broadcast

GIOVANNI PERGOLESI (1710-1736)

Lo frate 'nnamorato, Excerpt (Ogni pena più spietata)

Berlin November 1942	Raucheisen	LP: Melodiya M10 46863 008

Tre giorni son che Nina

Leipzig December 1956	Leipzig RO Fricke	Unpublished radio broadcast

HANS PFITZNER (1869-1949)

Die Rose vom Liebesgarten, Excerpt (Siegnots Waldmonolog)

Berlin June 1944	Städtische Oper Orchestra Schmidt-Isserstedt	Unpublished radio broadcast

Von deutscher Seele

Munich July 1952	Ebers, Pitzinger, Hotter Bavarian Radio Orchestra & Chorus Jochum	CD: Orfeo C273 922I

Urworte orphisch

Munich July 1952	Ebers, Pitzinger, Hotter Bavarian Radio Orchestra & Chorus Jochum	CD: Orfeo C273 922I

Lieder: Im tiefen Wald; Sonst; Ist der Himmel darum im Lenz so blau; Ich und du; Schön-Suschen

Stuttgart January 1960	Giesen	Unpublished radio broadcast

GIACOMO PUCCINI (1858-1924)

La Bohème, Excerpt (Dunque è proprio finita)

Berlin 1932	Berger, Oehme-Foerster, Domgraf-Fassbaender Staatskapelle Zaun <u>Sung in German</u>	78: Electrola EH 813/FKX 189

Madama Butterfly, Excerpt (Bimba dagli occhi/Viene la sera)

Berlin July 1937	Rudolph Reichssender and Deutschlandsender Orchestras Steiner Sung in German	Unpublished radio broadcast
Berlin 1943	Cebotari Berlin RO Rother Sung in German	45: Spezial EP 8040 LP: Saga XIG 8011 LP: Eterna 820 945/822 671-822 672 LP: Somerset 869 LP: DG 88 030 LP: BASF 22.21492-5/10.22142-3 LP: Vienna Disc TR 6248

Madama Butterfly, Excerpt (Addio fiorito asil)

Berlin February 1934	Hüsch Städtische Oper Orchestra Zaun Sung in German	78: Electrola EG 3035/EJ 119 LP: Electrola E 83385/WCLP 791 LP: Historia H 712-713 LP: Preiser LV 232 CD: Preiser 89088

Madama Butterfly, Excerpt (Dovunque al mondo)

Berlin February 1934	Hüsch Städtische Oper Orchestra Zaun Sung in German	78: Electrola EG 3035/EJ 119 LP: Electrola E 83385/WCLP 791 LP: Preiser LV 232 CD: Preiser 89088

Manon Lescaut, Excerpt (Donna non vidi mai)

Stuttgart June 1951	Württembergisches Staatsorchester Leitner	78: DG 62897 45: DG NL 32 073/EPL 30 490 LP: DG LPM 18 147
Stuttgart June 1951	Württembergisches Staatsorchester Leitner Sung in German	45: DG NL 32 072/EPL 30 489 LP: DG LPEM 19 043

Ludwig

MAX REGER (1873-1916)

Gebet

Hannover December 1956	Bohle	LP: DG LPEM 19 090
Stuttgart January 1958	Bohle	Unpublished radio broadcast

Herzenstausch

Berlin 1940	Peschko	78: Grammophon 47390
Berlin February 1943	Raucheisen	LP: Acanta 40.23565
Munich 1953	Altmann	Unpublished radio broadcast
Hannover November 1956	Bohle	LP: DG LPEM 19 090
Stuttgart January 1958	Bohle	Unpublished radio broadcast

Der Himmel hat eine Träne geweint

Hannover December 1956	Bohle	LP: DG LPEM 19 090
Stuttgart January 1958	Bohle	Unpublished radio broadcast

Im April

Hannover December 1956	Bohle	LP: DG LPEM 19 090
Stuttgart January 1958	Bohle	Unpublished radio broadcast

Reger Lieder/continued

Des Kindes Gebet

Berlin 1940	Peschko	78: Grammophon 47390
Hannover December 1956	Bohle	LP: DG LPEM 19090
Stuttgart January 1958	Bohle	Unpublished radio broadcast

Das kleinste Lied

Berlin February 1943	Raucheisen	LP: Acanta 40.23565
Hannover December 1956	Bohle	LP: DG LPEM 19 090
Stuttgart January 1958	Bohle	Unpublished radio broadcast

Mein Schätzelein

Berlin February 1943	Raucheisen	LP^Acanta 40.23565
Munich 1953	Altmann	Unpublished radio broadcast
Hannover November 1956	Bohle	LP: DG LPEM 19 090
Stuttgart January 1958	Bohle	Unpublished radio broadcast

Sag' es nicht, geliebtes Mädchen!

Hannover December 1956	Bohle	LP: DG LPEM 19 090

Ludwig

Reger Lieder/concluded

Schelmenliedchen

Munich 1953	Altmann	Unpublished radio broadcast
Hannover December 1956	Bohle	LP: DG LPEM 19 090
Stuttgart January 1958	Bohle	Unpublished radio broadcast

Viola d'amour

Hannover December 1956	Bohle	LP: DG LPEM 19 090
Stuttgart January 1958	Bohle	Unpublished radio broadcast

GIOACHINO ROSSINI (1792-1868)

Il barbiere di Siviglia

Stuttgart November 1937	<u>Role of Almaviva</u> Perras, Mayer, Bitterauf, Hann, Schmitt-Walter Reichssender Orchestra & Chorus Görlich <u>Sung in German</u>	Unpublished radio broadcast

Stabat mater

Cologne March 1953	Grümmer, Ilosvay, Fehn WDR Orchestra and Chorus Fricsay	CD: Melodram CDM 16523

La danza

Berlin December 1937	Kurzwellensender Orchestra Wicke	Unpublished radio broadcast

FRANZ SCHUBERT (1797-1828)

Die schöne Müllerin, Song cycle

Berlin December 1947	Puchelt	Unpublished radio broadcast <u>This recording is incomplete</u>
Stuttgart September 1949	Giesen	Unpublished radio broadcast
Berlin 1951	Raucheisen	78: DG 72189-72193 LP: DG LPM 18 031-18 032/ LPE 17 172-17 173 LP: Decca (USA) DL 9648 <u>Excerpts</u> LP: DG LPE 17 102

Abendlied

Hannover July 1958	Bohle	LP: DG LPM 18 034/SLPM 138 034

Am Strome (Ist mir's doch, als sei mein Lied)

Hamburg 1954	Brückner-Rüggeberg	Unpublished radio broadcast
Berlin May 1955	Raucheisen	DG unpublished
Hannover January 1956	Bohle	LP: DG LPEM 19 072

An den Frühling (Willkommen, schöner Jüngling!)

Stuttgart December 1956	Giesen	Unpublished radio broadcast
Hannover July 1958	Bohle	LP: DG LPEM 18 034/SLPM 138 034

An den Mond (Geuss', lieber Mond!)

Stuttgart December 1948	Giesen	Unpublished radio broadcast
Berlin May 1955	Raucheisen	DG unpublished
Hannover January 1956	Bohle	LP: DG LPEM 19 072
Munich 1956	Altmann	Unpublished radio broadcast

An die Laute (Leiser, leiser, kleine Laute)

Hannover July 1958	Bohle	LP: DG LPM 18 034/SLPM 138 034

An die Musik (Du holde Kunst, in wieviel grauen Stunden)

Stuttgart December 1948	Giesen	Unpublished radio broadcast

An eine Quelle (Du kleine grünumwachs'ne Quelle)

Berlin 1938	Vulté	Unpublished radio broadcast
Stuttgart December 1948	Giesen	Unpublished radio broadcast
Berlin May 1955	Raucheisen	DG unpublished
Hannover January 1956	Bohle	LP: DG LPEM 19 072

Ludwig

Schubert Lieder/continued

An Silvia (Was ist Silvia, saget an?)

Berlin 1938	Vulté	Unpublished radio broadcast
Berlin December 1944	Raucheisen	LP: Melodiya M10 46863 008
Stuttgart December 1948	Giesen	Unpublished radio broadcast
Hamburg 1954	Brückner-Rüggeberg	Unpublished radio broadcast
Hannover July 1958	Bohle	LP: DG LPM 18 034/SLPM 138 034

Auf dem See (Und frische Nahrung, neues Blut)

Berlin 1938	Vulté	Unpublished radio broadcast
Stuttgart May 1949	Giesen	Unpublished radio broadcast
Hamburg 1954	Brückner-Rüggeberg	Unpublished radio broadcast
Hannover July 1958	Bohle	LP: DG LPM 18 034/SLPM 138 034

Auf dem Wasser zu singen (Mitten im Schimmer der spiegelnden Wellen)

Stuttgart May 1949	Giesen	Unpublished radio broadcast
Berlin 1951	Raucheisen	78: DG 62884
Hannover July 1958	Bohle	LP: DG LPM 18 034/SLPM 138 034

Schubert Lieder/continued

Blumenlied (Es ist ein halbes Himmelreich)

Stuttgart December 1956	Giesen	Unpublished radio broadcast
Hannover July 1958	Bohle	LP: DG LPM 18 034/SLPM 138 034

Der Einsame (Wenn meine Grillen schwirren)

Berlin December 1944	Raucheisen	Unpublished radio broadcast
Stuttgart December 1948	Giesen	Unpublished radio broadcast
Hamburg 1954	Brückner-Rüggeberg	Unpublished radio broadcast
Berlin May 1955	Raucheisen	DG unpublished
Hannover January 1956	Bohle	LP: DG LPEM 19 092

Erntelied (Sicheln schallen, Aehren fallen)

Berlin December 1944	Raucheisen	LP: Melodiya M10 46863 008

Der Fischer (Das Wasser rauscht, das Wasser schwoll)

Hannover July 1958	Bohle	LP: DG LPM 18 034/SLPM 138 034

Das Fischermädchen/Schwanengesang (Du schönes Fischermädchen)

Hannover July 1958	Bohle	LP: DG LPM 18 034/SLPM 138 034

Ludwig

Schubert Lieder/continued
Fischerweise (Den Fischer fechten Sorgen)

Berlin 1951	Raucheisen	78: DG 72193
Berlin 1951	Raucheisen	78: DG 62884

Die Forelle (In einem Bächlein helle)

Berlin May 1955	Raucheisen	DG unpublished
Hannover January 1956	Bohle	LP: DG LPEM 19 072/LPEM 19 092

Frühlingsglaube (Die linden Düfte sind erwacht)

Stuttgart May 1949	Giesen	Unpublished radio broadcast
Hannover July 1958	Bohle	LP: DG LPM 18 034/SLPM 138 034/ 135 005/2545 032

Frühlingslied (Die Luft is blau, das Tal ist grün)

Hannover July 1958	Bohle	LP: DG LPM 18 034/SLPM 138 034

Frühlingssehnsucht/Schwanengesang (Säuselnde Lüfte wehend so mild)

Hannover July 1958	Bohle	LP: DG LPM 18 034/SLPM 138 034

Gott im Frühling (In seinem schimmernden Gewand)

Berlin May 1955	Raucheisen	DG unpublished
Hannover January 1965	Bohle	LP: DG LPEM 19 072

Schubert Lieder/continued

Der gute Hirte (Was sorgest du? Sei stille, meine Seele!)

Berlin May 1955	Raucheisen	DG unpublished
Hannover January 1956	Bohle	LP: DG LPEM 19 072

Heimliches Lieben (O du, wenn deine Lippen mich berühren)

Hamburg 1954	Brückner-Rüggeberg	Unpublished radio broadcast
Bremen April 1955	Bohle	Unpublished radio broadcast

Im Abendrot (O wie schön ist diese Welt)

Berlin December 1944	Raucheisen	LP: Melodiya M10 46863 008
Stuttgart December 1948	Giesen	Unpublished radio broadcast
Berlin 1952	Raucheisen	78: DG 62885 45: DG NL 32 033 LP: DG LPEM 19 127/9100/89 536
Hamburg 1954	Brückner-Rüggeberg	Unpublished radio broadcast

Im Frühling (Still sitz' ich an des Hügels Hang)

Hamburg 1954	Brückner-Rüggeberg	Unpublished radio broadcast
Hannover July 1958	Bohle	LP: DG LPM 18 034/SLPM 138 034/ 135 007/2545 032

Der Jüngling am Bache (An der Quelle sass der Knabe)

Stuttgart December 1956	Giesen	Unpublished radio broadcast

132 Ludwig

Schubert Lieder/continued

Der Jüngling an der Quelle (Leise, rieselnder Quell!)

Hannover July 1958	Bohle	LP: DG LPM 18 034/SLPM 138 034

Der Jüngling und der Tod (Die Sonne sinkt, o könnt' ich mit ihr scheiden)

Stuttgart December 1948	Giesen	Unpublished radio broadcast
Berlin 1952	Raucheisen	78: DG 62885 45: DG NL 32 033 LP: DG LPEM 19127/89 536

Liebesbotschaft/Schwanengesang (Rauschendes Bächlein, so silbern und hell)

Berlin May 1955	Raucheisen	DG unpublished
Hannover January 1956	Bohle	LP: DG LPEM 19 072

Das Lied im Grünen (Ins Grüne, ins Grüne, da lockt uns der Frühling)

Bremen April 1955	Bohle	Unpublished radio broadcast

Die Mutter Erde (Des Lebens Tag ist schwer und schwül)

Berlin May 1955	Raucheisen	DG unpublished
Hannover January 1956	Bohle	LP: DG LPEM 19 072

Sei mir gegrüsst (O du Entriss'ne mir und meinem Kusse!)

Bremen April 1955	Bohle	Unpublished radio broadcast

Schubert Lieder/continued

Ständchen (Horch, horch, die Lerch'!)

Stuttgart December 1948	Giesen	Unpublished radio broadcast

Ständchen/Schwanengesang (Leise flehen meine Lieder)

Berlin May 1955	Raucheisen	DG unpublished
Hannover January 1956	Bohle	LP: DG LPEM 19 072

Die Taubenpost/Schwanengesang (Ich hab' eine Brieftaub' in meinem Sold)

Hannover July 1958	Bohle	LP: DG LPM 18 034/SLPM 138 034

Vor meiner Wiege (Das also ist der enge Schrein)

Stuttgart December 1948	Giesen	Unpublished radio broadcast
Berlin 1951	Raucheisen	78: DG 72193 LP: DG LPEM 19 127/89 536

Der Wanderer an den Mond (Ich auf der Erd', am Himmel du!)

Hamburg 1954	Brückner-Rüggeberg	Unpublished radio broadcast
Berlin May 1955	Raucheisen	DG unpublished
Hannover January 1956	Bohle	LP: DG LPEM 19 072

134   Ludwig

Schubert Lieder/concluded

Wanderers Nachtlied (Der du von dem Himmel list)

Stuttgart   Giesen   Unpublished radio broadcast
May 1949

Was belebt die schöne Welt?

Stuttgart   Giesen   Unpublished radio broadcast
December 1956

Der Wegweiser/Winterreise (Was vermeid' ich denn die Wege?)

Berlin   Vulté   Unpublished radio broadcast
1938

HEINZ SCHUBERT (1908-1945)

Hymnisches Konzert

Berlin   Berger   LP: Melodiya M10 49723
December 1942   Heitmann, organ   CD: Melodiya MEL 10 00725
                  BPO   CD: Grammofono AB 78510
                  Furtwängler   CD: Hunt CDWFE 365

ROBERT SCHUMANN (1810-1856)

Szenen aus Goethes Faust

Berlin   L.Hoffman, Wolfram,   Unpublished radio broadcast
December 1944   Schmitt-Walter,
                  Nissen
                  Städtische Oper
                  Orchestra & Chorus
                  Schmidt-Isserstedt

Dichterliebe, Song cycle

Stuttgart March 1949	Giesen	Unpublished radio broadcast
Berlin 1951	Raucheisen	78: DG 72117-72118 LP: DG LP 16029/LPEM 19 127/89 536 LP: Decca (USA) DL 7525 LP: Atlas 6303

Auf einer Burg/Liederkreis op 39 (Eingeschlafen auf der Lauer)

Stuttgart March 1952	Giesen	Unpublished radio broadcast

Aufträge (Nicht so schnelle, nicht so schnelle!)

Hannover January 1956	Bohle	LP: DG LPEM 19 090

Frühlingsnacht/Liederkreis op 39 (Ueber Gärten durch die Lüfte)

Stuttgart March 1952	Giesen	Unpublished radio broadcast
Hannover January 1956	Bohle	LP: DG LPEM 19 090

Geisternähe (Was wider meine Schläfe)

Berlin 1942-1944	Raucheisen	LP: Melodiya M10 46863 008
Hannover January 1956	Bohle	LP: DG LPEM 19 090

Im Walde/Liederkreis op 39 (Es zog eine Hochzeit den Berg entlang)

Stuttgart March 1952	Giesen	Unpublished radio broadcast

Schumann Lieder/continued

In der Fremde I/Liederkreis op 39 (Aus der Heimat hinter den Blitzen rot)

Stuttgart March 1952	Giesen	Unpublished radio broadcast
Hannover November 1956	Bohle	LP: DG LPEM 19 090/LPEM 19 309

In der Fremde II/Liederkreis op 39 (Ich hör' die Bächlein rauschen)

Stuttgart March 1952	Giesen	Unpublished radio broadcast

Intermezzo/Liederkreis op 39 (Dein Bildnis wunderselig)

Berlin June 1943	Raucheisen	Unpublished radio broadcast
Stuttgart March 1952	Giesen	Unpublished radio broadcast
Hannover January 1956	Bohle	LP: DG LPEM 19 090

Mit Myrthen und Rosen/Liederkreis op 24

Hannover January 1956	Bohle	LP: DG LPEM 19 090

Mondnacht/Liederkreis op 39 (Es war, als hätt' der Himmel)

Stuttgart March 1952	Giesen	Unpublished radio broadcast
Hannover January 1956	Bohle	LP: DG LPEM 19 090/LPEM 19 309

Der Nussbaum (Es grünet ein Nussbaum vor dem Haus)

Hannover November 1956	Bohle	LP: DG LPEM 19 090

Schumann Lieder/concluded

Schöne Fremde/Liederkreis op 39 (Es rauschen die Wipfel und schauern)

Stuttgart March 1952	Giesen	Unpublished radio broadcast
Hannover November 1956	Bohle	LP: DG LPEM 19 090

Ständchen (Komm' in die stille Nacht)

Berlin 1942-1944	Raucheisen	LP: Melodiya M10 46863 008

Die Stille/Liederkreis op 39 (Es weiss und rät es doch keiner)

Stuttgart March 1952	Giesen	Unpublished radio broadcast

Waldesgespräch/Liederkreis op 39 (Es ist schon spät, es ist schon kalt)

Stuttgart March 1952	Giesen	Unpublished radio broadcast

Wehmut/Liederkreis op 39 (Ich kann wohl manchmal singen)

Stuttgart March 1952	Giesen	Unpublished radio broadcast

Zwielicht/Liederkreis op 39 (Dämm'rung will die Flügel spreiten)

Stuttgart March 1952	Giesen	Unpublished radio broadcast

BEDRICH SMETANA (1824-1884)

The Bartered Bride

Stuttgart April 1936	Role of Jenik Reining, Ducrue, Buchta, Hann Reichssender Orchestra & Chorus Zimmermann Sung in German	Unpublished radio broadcast
Cologne October 1950	E. Dietrich, Wilhelms, Hann WDR Orchestra and Chorus Lehmann Sung in German	Unpublished radio broadcast

The Bartered Bride, Excerpt (It must succeed!)

Berlin May 1942	Orchestra Steinkopf Sung in German	LP: BASF 22.21492-5/22.21486-9 LP: Historia H 673
Stuttgart July 1951	Württembergisches Staatsorchester Leitner Sung in German	78: DG LV 36 009 45: DG NL 32 202 LP: Eterna 821 075

The Bartered Bride, Excerpt (Just listen to me!/Give up your foolish love affair!)

Berlin January 1937	Strienz Staatskapelle Seidler-Winkler Sung in German	78: Electrola EH 1036 CD: Preiser 89089
Berlin May 1942	Hann Orchestra Steinkopf Sung in German	LP: BASF 22.21492-5/22.21486-9 LP: Historia H 665-666/H 673 LP: Bellaphon 620.05077 CD: ZYX Music PD 50372
Munich February 1954	Greindl Bavarian RO Lehmann Sung in German	45: DG EPL 30 554 LP: DG LPEM 19 014/LPEM 19 338/ SLPEM 136 338/89 637 LP: Eterna 820 130/821 075

The Bartered Bride, Excerpt (See the buds are bursting on the bushes)

Munich	Schlemm	45: DG EPL 30 302
February 1954	Bavarian Radio	LP: DG LPEM 19 014/LPEM 19 338/
	Orchestra & Chorus	SLPEM 136 338/89 637
	Lehmann	LP: Eterna 820 130
	Sung in German	

The Bartered Bride, Excerpt (So I find you here!)

Munich	Schlemm	45: DG EPL 30 145/EPL 30 302
February 1954	Bavarian RO	LP: DG LPEM 19 014/LPEM 19 338/
	Lehmann	SLPEM 136 338/89 637
	Sung in German	LP: Eterna 820 130

ALESSANDRO STRADELLA (1642-1682)

Pietà signore

Berlin	Raucheisen	LP: Melodiya M10 46863 008
October-		
November 1942		

OSCAR STRAUS (1870-1954)

Ein Walzertraum, Excerpt (Da draussen im duftigen Garten)

Munich	Bavaria SO	78: Polydor 48578
September 1951	Schmidt-Boelcke	

140 Ludwig

JOHANN STRAUSS II (1825-1899)

Eine Nacht in Venedig, Excerpt (Komm' in die Gondel)

Berlin December 1937	Kurzwellensender Orchestra Wicke	Unpublished radio broadcast
Berlin 1941	Staatskapelle and Chorus Steeger	78: Grammophon 47526

Der Zigeunerbaron

Stuttgart June 1936	Role of Barinkay Teschemacher, Mayer, Harlan, Hann, Buchta Reichssender Orchestra & Chorus Görlich	Unpublished radio broadcast

Der Zigeunerbaron, Potpourri

Berlin September 1936	Spletter, Pfahl, Arndt-Ober, Wrana, Kandl Reichssender Orchestras Steiner	Unpublished radio broadcast

Der Zigeunerbaron, Excerpt (Als flotter Geist)

Berlin December 1937	Kurzwellensender Orchestra Wicke	Unpublished radio broadcast

RICHARD STRAUSS (1864-1949)

Taillefer, Ballad for soloists, chorus and orchestra

Berlin November 1944	Cebotari, Hotter Lamy Choir Städtische Oper Orchestra Rother	LP: Urania UR 7042/US 7042 CD: Preiser 90222

Barkarole (Um der fallenden Ruder Spitzen)

Berlin February 1945	Raucheisen	LP: Acanta 40.23546

Cäcilie (Wenn du es wüsstest)

Berlin March 1934	Leitner	78: Electrola EG 3044 LP: Historia H 712-713
Berlin 1944	Orchestra Rother	Unpublished radio broadcast
Berlin February 1945	Raucheisen	LP: Acanta 40.23546

Du meines Herzens Krönelein

Munich December 1951– January 1952	Altmann	Unpublished radio broadcast
Berlin 1952	Raucheisen	Unpublished radio broadcast

Das Geheimnis (Du fragst mich, Mädchen)

Berlin February 1945	Raucheisen	Unpublished radio broadcast
Berlin 1952	Raucheisen	Unpublished radio broadcast

142 Ludwig

Strauss Lieder/continued

Heimkehr (Leiser schwanken die Aeste)

Stuttgart December 1948	Giesen	Unpublished radio broadcast
Berlin 1952	Raucheisen	Unpublished radio broadcast

Heimliche Aufforderung (Auf, hebe die funkelnde Schale empor!)

Munich December 1951- January 1952	Altmann	Unpublished radio broadcast

Ich trage meine Minne

Stuttgart December 1948	Giesen	Unpublished radio broadcast

Liebeshymnus (Heil jenem Tag!)

Berlin 1952	Raucheisen	Unpublished radio broadcast

Die Nacht (Aus dem Walde tritt die Nacht)

Berlin March 1934	Leitner	78: Electrola EG 3044
Berlin 1944	Raucheisen	LP: Acanta 40.23546 LP: Melodiya M10 46863 008
Stuttgart December 1948	Giesen	Unpublished radio broadcast
Berlin 1952	Raucheisen	LP: BASF 22.21807-4

Strauss Lieder/concluded

Nur Mut (Lass' das Zagen, trage mutig deine Sorgen!)

Berlin　　　　　　Raucheisen　　　　　　LP: Acanta 40.23546
February 1945

Seitdem dein Aug' in meines schaute

Berlin　　　　　　Raucheisen　　　　　　Unpublished radio broadcast
February 1945

Munich　　　　　　Altmann　　　　　　　Unpublished radio broadcast
December 1951–
January 1952

Berlin　　　　　　Raucheisen　　　　　　Unpublished radio broadcast
1952

Ständchen (Mach' auf, mach' auf, doch leise mein Kind!)

Berlin　　　　　　Raucheisen　　　　　　Unpublished radio broadcast
February 1945

Traum durch die Dämmerung (Weite Wiesen im Dämmergrau)

Munich　　　　　　Altmann　　　　　　　Unpublished radio broadcast
December 1951–
January 1952

Zueignung (Ja, du weisst es, teure Seele!)

Munich　　　　　　Altmann　　　　　　　Unpublished radio broadcast
December 1951–
January 1952

Berlin　　　　　　Raucheisen　　　　　　Unpublished radio broadcast
1952

144 Ludwig

FRANZ VON SUPPE (1819-1895)

Boccaccio, Querschnitt

Berlin March 1936	Frind, Strienz Orchestra & Chorus Seidler-Winkler	78: Electrola EH 919/FKX 73 LP: PR 10 CD: Centaur CRC 2116 The second side of this selection also appeared on Victor 78 36195

Boccaccio, Excerpt (Florenz hat schöne Frauen)

Berlin 1940	Claus Staatskapelle Steeger	78: Grammophon 15382 LP: Polydor LPHM 46677 LP: Historia H 712-713

PIOTR TCHAIKOVSKY (1840-1893)

Evgeny Onegin, Excerpt (Faint echo of my youth)

Munich 1948	Bavarian State Orchestra Leitner Sung in German	DG unpublished
Munich 1948	Bavarian State Orchestra Leitner Sung in German	78: DG 57342/68295
Munich May 1950	Bavarian RO Altmann Sung in German	LP: Allegro/Elite 3098 Pseudonyms used for participants on this recording
Munich 1951	Bavarian State Orchestra Leitner Sung in German	78: DG LV 36 001 LP: DG LPEM 19 023
Leipzig November 1956	Leipzig RO Stein Sung in German	Unpublished radio broadcast

AMBROISE THOMAS (1811-1896)

Mignon, Excerpt (Adieu Mignon)

Berlin	Städtische Oper	78: Electrola EH 810
September 1932	Orchestra	LP: Historia H 712-713
	Ladwig	LP: Preiser LV 232
	Sung in German	CD: Preiser 89088

GIUSEPPE VERDI (1813-1901)

Un ballo in maschera, Excerpt (Non sai tu che se l'anima mia)

Berlin	Teschemacher	78: Electrola EH 909
January 1935	Staatskapelle	LP: Preiser LV 63
	H-U.Müller	
	Sung in German	

La forza del destino, Excerpt (Ah, per sempre!)

Berlin	Teschemacher	78: Electrola EH 909
January 1935	Staatskapelle	LP: Preiser LV 63
	H-U.Müller	LP: Historia H 712-713
	Sung in German	

Rigoletto

Berlin	Role of Duke	Unpublished radio broadcast
October 1936	Berger, Heyer,	
	Reinmar, Rohr	
	Reichssender	
	Orchestra & Chorus	
	Steiner	
	Sung in German	

146 Ludwig

La Traviata, Querschnitt

Berlin November 1935	Role of Alfredo Perras, Hüsch, Staatskapelle and Chorus Seidler-Winkler Sung in German	78: Electrola EH 930/FKX 181 45: Electrola 7PW 550

La Traviata, Unspecified extracts

Munich 1951	Ebers, Schmitt-Walter Bavarian Radio Orchestra & Chorus Solti Sung in German	Unpublished radio broadcast

La Traviata, Excerpt (Libiamo ne' lieti calici)

Berlin 1943	Cebotari Berlin RO Rother Sung in German	Unpublished radio broadcast

La Traviata, Excerpt (E strano!/Ah forse è lui!/Follie! Sempre libera!)

Berlin 1943	Cebotari Berlin RO Rother Sung in German	45: DG EPL 30 531 LP: DG 88 016 LP: Saga FID 2143 LP: Eterna 520 094 LP: BASF 22.21483-21484/22.21492-5 LP: Historia H 712-713 CD: Preiser 90248

La Traviata, Excerpt (Dei miei bollenti spiriti)

Leipzig January 1957	Leipzig RO Masur Sung in German	Unpublished radio broadcast

La Traviata, Excerpt (Parigi o cara)

Berlin	Cebotari	45: DG EPL 30 531
1943	Berlin RO	LP: DG 88 016
	Rother	LP: Saga FID 2143
	<u>Sung in German</u>	LP: Eterna 520 094
		LP: BASF 22.21483-21484/22.21492-5
		LP: Historia H 677-678/H 712-713
		CD: Preiser 90248

Il Trovatore, Excerpt (Condotta ell' era in ceppi/Ai nostri monti)

Stuttgart	Höngen	78: DG 72120
May 1951	Württembergisches	LP: DG LPM 18 047/LPEM 19 029
	Staatsorchester	LP: Preiser 1111 165
	Leitner	
	<u>Sung in German</u>	

Requiem

Munich	Cunitz, Höngen,	LP: Melodram MEL 232
December 1950	Greindl	CD: Orfeo C195 892I
	Bavarian Radio	
	Orchestra & Chorus	
	Jochum	

RICHARD WAGNER (1813-1883)

Tannhäuser, Excerpt (So ist's! Gepriesen sei das Lied!/Ein furchtbares Verbrechen ward hier begangen!)

Berlin	<u>Role of Walther</u>	LP: BASF 22.22199-9
November-	<u>von der Vogelweide</u>	LP: Acanta 40.23502
December 1942	Reining, Lorenz,	
	L.Hofmann,	
	Schmitt-Walter,	
	Grossmann	
	Städtische Oper	
	Chorus	
	Berlin RO	
	Rother	

148   Ludwig

CARL MARIA VON WEBER (1786-1826)

Der Freischütz, Querschnitt

| Berlin
March 1936 | Role of Max
Frind, Strienz
Staatskapelle
and Chorus
Seidler-Winkler | 78: Electrola EH 963/FKX 179 |

Der Freischütz, Excerpt (Durch die Wälder, durch die Auen)

| Königsberg
February 1940 | Reichssender
Orchestra
Wöller | Unpublished radio broadcast |

Oberon

| Berlin
August 1938 | Role of Oberon
Teschemacher,
Schilp, Rosvaenge,
Schmitt-Walter
Reichssender
Orchestra & Chorus
Rosbaud | Unpublished radio broadcast |

FELIX VON WEINGARTNER (1863-1942)

Liebesfeier

| Berlin
November 1934 | Leitner | 78: Electrola EG 3242 |

RICHARD WETZ

Lieder: Die Muschel; Juli; Das Meer ist für die Fischer; Beichtiger

| Bremen
1955 | Bohle | Unpublished radio broadcast |

HUGO WOLF (1860-1903)

Der Corregidor, Excerpt (Herz, verzage nicht geschwind!)

Stuttgart April 1951	Württembergisches Staatsorchester Leitner	78: DG 62886 45: DG NL 32 209

Abschied/Mörike-Lieder (Unangeklopft ein Herr tritt abends bei mir an)

Berlin 1952	Raucheisen	Unpublished radio broadcast
Munich 1957	Altmann	Unpublished radio broadcast

An die Geliebte/Mörike-Lieder (Wenn ich, vor deinem Anschau'n tief gestillt)

Berlin January 1943	Raucheisen	LP: Acanta 40.23580
May 1958	Faender	Unpublished radio broadcast

Anakreons Grab/Goethe-Lieder (Wo die Rose hier blüht)

Vienna November 1948	Werba	Columbia unpublished
Vienna February 1949	Nordberg	Columbia unpublished

Auch kleine Dinge/Italienisches Liederbuch

Berlin November 1938	Vulté	Unpublished radio broadcast
Berlin 1940	Peschko	78: Grammophon 47374

STAATSOPER
IM THEATER AN DER WIEN

Mittwoch, den 10. März 1948

Der Barbier von Sevilla

Komische Oper in zwei Akten
Text nach Beaumarchais von Cesare Sterbini
Musik von Gioacchino Rossini
Musikalische Leitung: Wilhelm Loibner
Inszenierung: Erich Wymetal

Graf Almaviva	* * *
Doktor Bartolo	Alfred Jerger
Rosine, dessen Mündel	Rosl Schwaiger
Basilio, Musikmeister	Marjan Rus
Berta, Gouvernante der Rosine	Else Schürhoff
Figaro, Barbier	Giuseppe Taddei
Fiorillo, des Grafen Diener	Ljubomir Pantscheff
Ein Offizier	Harald Pröglhöf
Ein Notar	Hans Kres
Ambrosio, Bartolos Diener	Lothar Höberth

Musikanten, Soldaten

Ort der Handlung: Sevilla — Zeit: Mitte des 18. Jahrhunderts

* * * „Graf Almaviva" Walther Ludwig a. G.

Einlage im zweiten Akt: Donizetti: „Linda von Chamounix",
gesungen von Rosl Schwaiger

Nach dem ersten Akt eine größere Pause

Kasseneröffnung 17½ Uhr   Anfang 18½ Uhr   Ende etwa 20¾ Uhr

Spielplan:

Donnerstag 11. März. Don Giovanni (Anfang 18½ Uhr)
Freitag 12. März. Rigoletto (Anfang 18½ Uhr)
Samstag 13. März. Dantons Tod (Anfang 18½ Uhr)
Sonntag 14. März. Nachmittags 14 Uhr: Die Entführung aus dem Serail.
Geschl. Vorstellung f. d. „Theater d. Jugend". Kein Kartenverkauf
Abends 18½ Uhr: La Traviata
Im Redoutensaal: Così fan tutte (Anfang 18½ Uhr)

Der Kartenvorverkauf findet an der Tageskasse I., Bräunerstraße 14
(Tel. R 28 5 65), statt

Preis des Programmes 50 Groschen

SALZBURGER FESTSPIELE 1949

VIERTES ORCHESTERKONZERT

DIE WIENER PHILHARMONIKER

UNTER DER LEITUNG VON

HERBERT KARAJAN

MITWIRKEND:

IRMGARD SEEFRIED (SOPRAN)
ELISABETH HÖNGEN (ALT)
WALTER LUDWIG (TENOR)
BORIS CHRISTOFF (BASS)

SINGVEREIN DER GESELLSCHAFT DER MUSIKFREUNDE

152 Ludwig

Wolf Lieder/continued

Auf einer Wanderung/Mörike-Lieder (In ein freundliches Städtchen tret'ich ein)

Munich 1957	Altmann	Unpublished radio broadcast

Begegnung/Mörike-Lieder (Was doch heut' nacht ein Sturm gewesen)

Stuttgart December 1948	Giesen	Unpublished radio broadcast
Berlin 1952	Raucheisen	Unpublished radio broadcast
Munich 1957	Altmann	Unpublished radio broadcast

Denk' es, o Seele!/Mörike-Lieder (Ein Tännlein grünet wo)

Stuttgart May 1948	Giesen	Unpublished radio broadcast
Munich 1957	Altmann	Unpublished radio broadcast

Dies zu deuten bin ich erbötig/Goethe-Lieder

Berlin 1952	Raucheisen	Unpublished radio broadcast

Erschaffen und Beleben/Goethe-Lieder (Hans Adam war ein Erdenkloss)

Berlin 1952	Raucheisen	Unpublished radio broadcast

Der Freund/Eichendorff-Lieder (Wer auf den Wogen schliefe)

Munich 1957	Altmann	Unpublished radio broadcast

Wolf Lieder/continued

Frech und froh I & II/Goethe-Lieder (Mit Mädchen sich vertragen; Liebesqual verschmäht mein Herz)

Berlin   Raucheisen   LP: Acanta 40.23580
January 1943

Frühling übers Jahr/Goethe-Lieder (Das Beet schon lockert sich in die Höh')

Berlin   Raucheisen   LP: Acanta 40.23580
January 1943

May   Faender   Unpublished radio broadcast
1958

Fussreise/Mörike-Lieder (Am frischgeschnitt'nen Wanderstab)

Stuttgart   Giesen   Unpublished radio broadcast
December 1948

Berlin   Raucheisen   Unpublished radio broadcast
1952

Munich   Altmann   Unpublished radio broadcast
1957

Der Gärtner/Mörike-Lieder (Auf ihrem Leibrösslein so weiss wie der Schnee)

Berlin   Raucheisen   LP: Acanta 40.23580
January 1943

May   Faender   Unpublished radio broadcast
1958

Ganymed/Goethe-Lieder (Wie im Morgenglanze du rings mich anglühst)

Berlin   Raucheisen   LP: Acanta 40.23580
January 1943

Ludwig

Wolf Lieder/continued

Gebet/Mörike-Lieder (Herr, schicke was du willst)

Stuttgart May 1948	Giesen	Unpublished radio broadcast
Berlin 1952	Raucheisen	Unpublished radio broadcast
Munich 1957	Altmann	Unpublished radio broadcast

Der Genesene an die Hoffnung/Mörike-Lieder (Tödlich graute mir der Morgen)

Munich 1957	Altmann	Unpublished radio broadcast

Gesegnet sei, durch den die Welt entstund/Italienisches Liederbuch

Vienna November 1948	Werba	Columbia unpublished

Gesellenlied (Kein Meister fällt vom Himmel!)

Stuttgart December 1948	Giesen	Unpublished radio broadcast
Vienna February 1949	Nordberg	Columbia unpublished
Berlin 1952	Raucheisen	Unpublished radio broadcast
Berlin 1956	Bohle	45: Eterna 520 093

Heimweh/Eichendorff-Lieder (Wer in die Fremde will wandern)

Stuttgart May 1948	Giesen	Unpublished radio broadcast
Munich 1957	Altmann	Unpublished radio broadcast

Wolf Lieder/continued

Herz, verzage nicht geschwind!/Spanisches Liederbuch

Berlin   Raucheisen   LP: Acanta 40.23581
March 1943

Der Jäger/Mörike-Lieder (Drei Tage Regen fort und fort)

Berlin   Raucheisen   LP: Acanta 40.23580
January 1943

Komm', Liebchen, komm', umwinde mir die Mütze/Goethe-Lieder

Berlin   Raucheisen   LP: Acanta 40.23580
January 1943

Berlin   Raucheisen   Unpublished radio broadcast
1952

May   Faender   Unpublished radio broadcast
1958

Locken, haltet mich gefangen/Goethe-Lieder

Berlin   Raucheisen   LP: Acanta 40.23580
January 1943

Der Musikant/Eichendorff-Lieder (Wandern lieb' ich für mein Leben)

Stuttgart   Giesen   Unpublished radio broadcast
December 1948

Berlin   Bohle   45: Eterna 520 093
1956

Munich   Altmann   Unpublished radio broadcast
1957

156 Ludwig

Wolf Lieder/continued

Seemanns Abschied/Eichendorff-Lieder (Ade, mein Schatz!)

Munich 1957	Altmann	Unpublished radio broadcast

Solang man nüchtern ist/Goethe-Lieder

Berlin January 1943	Raucheisen	LP: Acanta 40.23580
Berlin 1952	Raucheisen	Unpublished radio broadcast
May 1958	Faender	Unpublished radio broadcast

Das Ständchen/Eichendorff-Lieder (Auf die Dächer zwischen blassen Wolken)

Vienna February 1949	Nordberg	Columbia unpublished
Munich 1957	Altmann	Unpublished radio broadcast

Storchenbotschaft/Mörike-Lieder (Des Schäfers sein Haus und das steht auf zwei Rad)

Berlin April 1943	Raucheisen	LP: Acanta 40.23580
Berlin December 1944	Raucheisen	Unpublished radio broadcast
Berlin 1956	Bohle	45: Eterna 520 093

Der Tambour/Mörike-Lieder (Wenn meine Mutter hexen könnt'!)

Berlin 1952	Raucheisen	Unpublished radio broadcast
Berlin 1956	Bohle	45: Eterna 520 093
Munich 1957	Altmann	Unpublished radio broadcast

Wolf Lieder/continued

Nicht Gelegenheit macht Diebe/Goethe-Lieder

Berlin January 1943	Raucheisen	LP: Acanta 40.23580
Berlin 1952	Raucheisen	Unpublished radio broadcast

Nimmersatte Liebe/Mörike-Lieder (So ist die Lieb'!)

Berlin 1940	Peschko	78: Grammophon 47374 LP: Historia H 712-713
Berlin January 1943	Raucheisen	LP: Acanta 40.23580
Stuttgart December 1948	Giesen	Unpublished radio broadcast
Berlin 1952	Raucheisen	Unpublished radio broadcast
Munich 1957	Altmann	Unpublished radio broadcast
May 1958	Faender	Unpublished radio broadcast

Nun lass uns Frieden schliessen/Italienisches Liederbuch

Vienna November 1948	Werba	Columbia unpublished

Ob der Koran von Ewigkeit sei?/Goethe-Lieder

Berlin 1952	Raucheisen	Unpublished radio broadcast

Der Scholar/Eichendorff-Lieder (Bei dem angenehmen Wetter)

Munich 1957	Altmann	Unpublished radio broadcast

Ludwig

Wolf Lieder/concluded

Trunken müssen wir alle sein/Goethe-Lieder

Berlin   Raucheisen   LP: Acanta 40.23580
January 1943

Und willst du deinen Liebsten sterben sehen/Italienisches Liederbuch

Berlin   Vulté   Unpublished radio broadcast
November 1938

Unfall/Eichendorff-Lieder (Ich ging bei Nacht einst über Land)

Munich   Altmann   Unpublished radio broadcast
1957

Verborgenheit/Mörike-Lieder (Lass', o Welt, o lass' mich sein!)

Munich   Altmann   Unpublished radio broadcast
1957

Berlin   Bohle   LP: Electrola E 83385/WCLP 791
November 1962

Was in der Schenke waren heute/Goethe-Lieder

Berlin   Raucheisen   LP: Acanta 40.23580
January 1943

Wer sein holdes Lieb verloren/Spanisches Liederbuch

Berlin   Raucheisen   LP: Acanta 40.23581
March 1943

Berlin   Weitzmann   Unpublished radio broadcast
December 1956

CARL ZELLER (1842-1898)

Der Vogelhändler, Excerpt (Schenkt man sich Rosen im Tirol)

Berlin September 1934	Jungkurth Staatskapelle and Chorus Schönbaumsfeld	78: Electrola EH 893/FKX 84
Berlin July 1937	Rudolph Reichssender and Deutschlandsender Orchestras Steiner	Unpublished radio broadcast
Berlin 1940	Claus Staatskapelle and Chorus Steeger	78: Grammophon 15338

WALTHER LUDWIG PERFORMS SONGS FROM FILMS OF THE THIRTIES

Bella fiametta, from the film Boccaccio

Berlin   Orchestra   78: Electrola EG 3659
March 1936   Seidler-Winkler

Bella Venezia, from the film Ein gewisser Herr Grau

Berlin   Orchestra   78: Electrola EG 2842/BA 391
1932   Rüth   LP: Historia H 712-713

Es gibt nur eine Liebe, from the film of the same title

Berlin   Orchestra   78: Electrola EG 2880
1932   Rüth

Heute abend bei mir, from the film of the same title

Berlin   Orchestra   78: Electrola EG 3036
March 1934   Buschkötter

Heute nacht oder nie, from the film Das Lied einer Nacht

Berlin   Orchestra   78: Electrola EG 2555/EG 2623
1932   Rüth

Ich hab' dich lieb und muss es dir sagen, from the film Herz über Bord

Berlin   Orchestra   78: Electrola EG 3246
December 1934   Marszalek

Ich sehn' mich nach dir, from the film of the same title

Berlin   Orchestra   78: Electrola EG 3185
November 1934   Schönbaumsfeld

Songs from films of the Thirties/continued

Ich sing' mein Lied heut' nur für dich, from the film Mein Herz ruft nach dir

Berlin	Orchestra	78: Electrola EG 3030
March 1934	Buschkötter	

Ich trage stets dein Bild im Herzen, from the film Ist mein Mann nicht fabelhaft?

Berlin	Orchestra	78: Electrola EG 2879
1932	Rüth	

Mein Herz ruft immer nur nach dir, from the film of the same title

Berlin	Orchestra	78: Electrola EG 3030
March 1934	Buschkötter	

Mein Himmel auf Erden, from the film Himmel auf Erden

Berlin	Orchestra	78: Electrola EG 3420
1935	Seidler-Winkler	

Ob blond oder braun, from the film Ich lieb' alle Frauen

Berlin	Orchestra	78: Electrola EG 3427
August 1935		

Romantische Nächte, from the film Boccaccio

Berlin	Orchestra	78: Electrola EG 3659
March 1936	Seidler-Winkler	

Schenk' mir dein Herz heute nacht, from the film Ich lieb' alle Frauen

Berlin	Orchestra	78: Electrola EG 3427
August 1935		

162 Ludwig

Songs from films of the Thirties/continued

Ein Tag ohne dich, from the film 8 Mädels im Boot

Berlin September 1932	Tanzorchester Marek Weber <u>Ludwig sings anonymously on this recording</u>	78: Electrola EG 2621

Die Tage vergeh'n, from the film Die Freundin eines grossen Mannes

Berlin February 1934	Funk-Orchester Müller	78: Electrola EG 2983 LP: Historia H 712-713

Tausend rote Rosen blüh'n, from the film Ein Walzer für dich

Berlin May 1934	Orchestra Dobrindt	78: Electrola EG 3060 LP: Hansa 204 844.241

Tausendmal war ich im Traum bei dir, from the film Amphitryon

Berlin 1935	Orchestra Seidler-Winkler	78: Electrola EG 3420

Turandot, bezaubernde Turandot!, from the film Prinzessin Turandot

Berlin November 1934	Orchestra Schönbaumsfeld	78: Electrola EG 3185

Unsere Zeit ist gekommen, from the film Der Rebell

Berlin 1932	Orchestra Goehr	78: Electrola EG 2729

Wenn das Herz auch bricht, from the film Herz über Bord

Berlin December 1934	Orchestra Marszalek	78: Electrola EG 3246

Songs from films of the Thirties/concluded

Wenn du nicht kommst, from the film Ich bei Tag und du bei Nacht

Berlin	Orchestra	78: Electrola EG 2686
1932	Sommer	

Willst du ein bisschen Glück an mich verschenken, from the film Die Tänzerin von Sanssouci

Berlin	Tanzorchester	78: Electrola EG 2621
September 1932	Marek Weber	
	<u>Ludwig sings anonymously on this recording</u>	

164 Ludwig

MISCELLANEOUS, TRADITIONAL AND FOLKSONGS

Durch Oper und Operette: Grosses Electrola-Künstlertreffen

Berlin	Frind, Perras,	78: Electrola EH 945
November 1935	Jungkurth, Korjus,	LP: OASI-556
	Klose, Wittrisch,	CD: Centaur CRC 2116
	Hüsch, Strienz	

Ach du liebes Mägdlein!

Berlin	Orchestra	78: Electrola EG 2729
1932	Goehr	

Ach, wie ist's möglich dann?

Berlin	Berlin RO	LP: DG LPE 17 111
November 1957	Gaebel	

Aennchen von Tharau

Berlin	Berlin String	78: Electrola EG 3364
January 1935	Quartet	
	Seidler-Winkler, piano	
Berlin	Berlin RO	LP: DG LPE 17 111
November 1957	Gaebel	

Am Brunnen vor dem Tore

Berlin	Berlin RO	LP: DG LPE 17 111/136 326
November 1957	Gaebel	LP: Polydor SLPHM 237 240

Anita-Serenade

Berlin	Orchestra	78: Electrola EG 2880
1932	Rüth	

Miscellaneous, Traditional and Folksongs/continued

Buona notte, schöne Signorina!

Berlin 1932	Orchestra Sommer	78: Electrola EG 2686

Capri-Serenade

Berlin 1935	Orchestra Marszalek	78: Electrola EG 3370/JK 2557

Chianti-Lied

Berlin 1941	Staatskapelle and Chorus Steeger	78: Grammophon 47526

Christnacht

Berlin 1938	Instrumentalists	78: Grammophon 47258

Deutsche Werkhymne

Berlin 1932	Städtische Oper Orchestra & Chorus Heger	78: Electrola EH 833/EH 839

Deutschland, du darfst nicht untergeh'n!

Berlin 1932	Orchestra Urack	78: Electrola EG 2813

166 Ludwig

Miscellaneous, Traditional and Folksongs/continued

Drauss' ist alles so prächtig

Berlin January 1935	Berlin String Quartet Seidler-Winkler, piano	78: Electrola EG 3329
Berlin 1944	Orchestra Steinkopf	Unpublished radio broadcast
Berlin November 1957	Berlin RO Gaebel	LP: DG LPE 17 111

Du, du liegst mir im Herzen

Berlin November 1957	Berlin RO Gaebel	LP: DG LPE 17 111

Du erinnerst mich an meine erste Liebe

Berlin September 1932	Tanzorchester Marek Weber <u>Ludwig sings anonymously on this recording</u>	78: Electrola EG 2632

Einmal

Berlin 1932	Orchester Rüth	78: Electrola EG 2555

Erlaube mir, Feinsliebchen!

Berlin 1944	Orchestra Steinkopf	Unpublished radio broadcast

Fidele Sänger am Rhein, Potpourri

Berlin November 1934	Frind, Strienz Orchestra & Chorus Seidler-Winkler	78: Electrola EH 903

Miscellaneous, Traditional and Folksongs/continued

Der Flug zum Niederwald

Berlin April 1936	Deutschlander Orchestra Jahn	Unpublished radio broadcast

Der goldene Pierrot, Querschnitt

Berlin 1934	Scholwer Orchestra Schönbaumsfeld	78: Electrola EH 872

Heimat, du Inbegriff der Liebe!

Berlin March 1934	Orchestra Dobrindt	78: Electrola EG 3016 LP: Historia H 712-713

Das Herz am Rhein

Berlin September 1940	Deutschlandsender Orchestra & Chorus Steinkopf	Unpublished radio broadcast

Holunderblüten und Maiennacht

Berlin March 1934	Orchestra Dobrindt	78: Electrola EG 3016

Hörst du mein Lied?

Berlin December 1934	Orchestra	78: Electrola EG 3221

Im Wald und auf der Heide, Potpourri

Berlin 1935	Orchestra Favre Choir Seidler-Winkler	78: Electrola EH 928

168 Ludwig

Miscellaneous, Traditional and Folksongs/continued

In einem kühlen Grunde

Berlin	Berlin String	78: Electrola EG 3364
January 1935	Quartet	
	Seidler-Winkler, piano	

| Berlin | Berlin RO | LP: DG LPE 17 111 |
| November 1957 | Gaebel | LP: Polydor SLPHM 237 244 |

Isola bella

| Berlin | Orchestra | 78: Electrola EG 3036/EG 3039 |
| 1934 | Schönbaumsfeld | |

Kleine Liebesgeschichte

Berlin	Zöbisch, Hölger,	78: Electrola EG 2862-2863
1932	Orchestra	
	Rüth	

Lieb' mich im 3/4 Takt, Potpourri

Berlin	Frind	78: Electrola EG 2975
December 1933	Orchestra	
	Ettlinger	

Lobetanz

Berlin	Callem	Unpublished radio broadcast
May 1935	Funkorchester	Surviving recording is incomplete
	Frickhöffer	

Lucrezia-Barkarole

| Berlin | Orchestra | 78: Electrola EG 3370/JK 2557 |
| 1935 | Marszalek | |

Miscellaneous, Traditional and Folksongs/continued

Lustige Studenten, Potpourri

Berlin	Frind, Strienz	78: Electrola EG 3232
December 1934	Orchestra & Chorus	78: Victor 25-4036
	Seidler-Winkler	

Mariagneta

Berlin	Leitner	78: Grammophon 62824
1941		

Marie-Luise

Berlin	Orchestra	78: Electrola EG 2842/BA 391
1932	Rüth	LP: Historia H 712-713

Melodie der Liebe

Berlin	Orchestra	78: Electrola EG 2879
1932	Rüth	

Morgen muss ich fort von hier!

Berlin	Berlin RO	LP: DG LPE 17 111
November 1957	Gaebel	

O du fröhliche!

Berlin	Instrumentalists	78: Grammophon 47257
1938		78: Supraphon C 191140

Ob du mich wirklich lieb hast?/Zigeunerträume

Berlin	Tanzorchester	78: Electrola EG 2608
1932	Marek Weber	
	<u>Ludwig sings anonymously on this recording</u>	

Ludwig

Miscellaneous, Traditional and Folksongs/continued

Schlaf wohl, du Himmelknabe du!

Berlin 1938	Instrumentalists	78: Grammophon 47258

Serenata veneziana

Berlin February 1936	Deutschlandsender Orchestra Melichar	Unpublished radio broadcast

Siehst du im Osten das Morgenrot?

Berlin 1932	Orchestra Urack	78: Electrola EG 2813

Tausend Sterne leuchten

Berlin February 1934	Funkorchester Müller	78: Electrola EG 2983

Und der Hans schleicht umher

Berlin November 1957	Berlin RO Gaebel	LP: DG LPE 17 111

Verbotener Gesang

Berlin December 1937	Kurzwellensender Orchestra Wicke	Unpublished radio broadcast

Was hab' ich denn meinem Feinsliebchen getan?

Berlin November 1957	Berlin RO Gaebel	LP: DG LPE 17 111

Miscellaneous, Traditional and Folksongs/concluded

Die weissen Wolken wandern

Berlin	Orchestra	78: Electrola EG 3221
November 1934	Schönbaumsfeld	

Zigeuner, du hast mein Herz gestohlen!

Berlin	Tanzorchester	78: Electrola EG 2633
April 1932	Marek Weber	
	<u>Ludwig sings anonymously on this recording</u>	

CINEMA FILMS WITH WALTHER LUDWIG

Ich bei Tag und du bei Nacht
1932/directed by Ludwig Beyer
Co-star Ursula van Diemen

Der Weg ins Freie
1941/directed by Rolf Hansen
Walther Ludwig sings extracts from Rigoletto and Mackeben's Der Stern hat uns gefunden.
Other singers include Zarah Leander and Hans Reinmar.

Fritz Wunderlich
1930-1966

Discography compiled
by John Hunt

HANS ANDERS

Nacht überm See

Freiburg September 1954	Südwestfunk Orchestra Stech	Unpublished radio broadcast

Wenn der Mund schweigt; Wolken geh'n am Himmel

Kaiserslautern June 1954	Südwestfunk Orchestra Smola	Unpublished radio broadcast

JOHANN SEBASTIAN BACH (1685-1750)

Cantata No 21 "Ich hatte viel Bekümmernis"

Stuttgart 1955	Sailer, H.Münch, Titze Stuttgart Soloists and Chorus Couraud	LP: Discophile française DF 180 LP: Schallplattengilde Wien AGL 107

Cantata No 31 "Der Himmel lacht, die Erde jubilieret"

Stuttgart January- March 1956	Sailer, Bence Messthaler Stuttgart Soloists and Chorus Couraud	LP: Discophile française LP: Philips (France) 77410 LP: Philips (Germany) L09399L <u>For contractual reasons Wunderlich sings on this recording under the name of Werner S.Braun</u>

Cantata No 208 "Was mir behagt, ist die muntere Jagd"

Berlin November 1961	Kupper, Köth, Fischer-Dieskau St.Hedwig's Choir Berlin SO Forster	LP: Electrola E 70475/STE 70475 LP: HMV ALP 1985/ASD 534 LP: EMI 1C 063 28160/ED 29 03701

Christmas Oratorio

Stuttgart December 1958	Sailer, Winkler, Swedberg SDR Orchestra and Chorus Langenbeck	Unpublished radio broadcast

Berlin
February-
June 1965
	Janowitz, C.Ludwig,
	Crass
	Munich Bach
	Orchestra & Chorus
	K.Richter
		LP: DG APM 14 353-14 355/
		    SAPM 198 353-198 355/2710 004/
		    2722 018/2723 063
		CD: DG 413 6252/427 2362
		Excerpts
		LP: DG 136 498/199 039/2535 369
		Rehearsal extracts also published on
		a promotional LP

Easter Oratorio

Stuttgart January- March 1956	Sailer, Bence, Messthaler Stuttgart Soloists and Chorus Couraud	LP: Discophile française LP: Philips (France) 77412 LP: Philips (Germany) 835 498AY For contractual reasons Wunderlich sings on this recording under the name of Werner S.Braun

Magnificat

Stuttgart January- March 1956	Sailer, Bence, Messthaler Stuttgart Soloists and Chorus Couraud	LP: Discophile française LP: Philips (France) 77410 LP: Philips (Germany) L09399L For contractual reasons Wunderlich sings on this recording under the name of Werner S.Braun

Mass in B minor

Stuttgart September 1956	Stader, Höffgen, Rehfuss Freiburg Bach Choir Winterthur Stadtorchester Egel	Unpublished radio broadcast
Stuttgart 1959	Sailer, Bence, Wenk Schwäbischer Singkreis Stuttgart Pro Musica Orchestra Grischkat	LP: Vox VBX 7/SVBX 57/STPL 511283 LP: Eurodisc XDK 80010

Saint Matthew Passion

Vienna April 1962	<u>Evangelist and tenor arias</u> Lipp, C.Ludwig, Wiener, Berry Wiener Singverein VSO Böhm	Unpublished radio broadcast
Ludwigsburg July 1964	<u>Tenor arias</u> Ameling, Höffgen, Pears, Prey, Krause Stuttgart Chamber Orchestra & Chorus Münchinger	LP: Decca MET 288-291/SET 288-291 CD: Decca 414 0572 <u>Excerpts</u> LP: Decca LXT 6272/SXL 6272 CD: Decca 443 3792/448 6892

Saint John Passion

Freiburg February 1958	<u>Evangelist</u> Giebel, Höffgen, Rotsch, Günter, Rehfuss Südwestfunk Orchestra & Chorus Freiburg Bach Choir Egel	Unpublished radio broadcast
Berlin September 1961	Grümmer, Otto, Traxel, Kohn, Fischer-Dieskau St.Hedwig's Choir Berlin SO Forster	LP: Electrola E 80668-80670/ STE 80668-80670 LP: HMV ALP 1975-1977/ASD 526-528 LP: EMI 1C 147 28589-28591 CD: EMI CMS 764 2342 <u>Excerpts</u> LP: Electrola E 80727/STE 80727

DIETRICH VON BAUSZNERN

Jaqueline Putputput, opera for radio

Freiburg July 1954	Mikulicz-Radecki, Harlan Freiburg Hochschule Orchestra & Chorus Wich	Unpublished radio broadcast

LUDWIG VAN BEETHOVEN (1770-1827)

Adelaide (Einsam wandelt dein Freund im Frühlingsgarten)

Mainz November 1962	Reinhardt	Unpublished radio broadcast
Schwetzingen May 1965	Giesen	Unpublished radio broadcast
Salzburg August 1965	Giesen	LP: Acanta 40.23529 CD: Acanta 43.529
Munich October- November 1965	Giesen	LP: DG LPEM 39 125/SLPEM 139 125/ 2535 614/2721 230/413 8371 CD: DG 429 9332/435 1452/447 9212
Hannover March 1966	Giesen	CD: Bella voce BV 107.003 CD: Myto MCD 93278
Edinburgh September 1966	Giesen	Unpublished radio broadcast

An die ferne Geliebte, song cycle

Vienna May 1963	H. Schmidt	LP: Philips 6520 022 CD: Philips 420 8522

Andenken (Ich denke dein)

Stuttgart 1956	Reinhardt	LP: Europäischer Fonoklub 4304 LP: Eurodisc OK 25290

Der Kuss (Ich war bei Chloen ganz allein)

Schwetzingen May 1965	Giesen	Unpublished radio broadcast
Salzburg August 1965	Giesen	LP: Acanta 40.23529 CD: Acanta 43.529
Munich October- November 1965	Giesen	LP: DG LPEM 39 125/SLPEM 139 125/ 2535 614/413 8371 CD: DG 429 9332/435 1452/447 9212
Hannover March 1966	Giesen	CD: Bella voce BV 107.003 CD: Myto MCD 93278
Edinburgh September 1966	Giesen	Unpublished radio broadcast

Mailied (Wie herrlich leuchtet mir die Natur)

Stuttgart 1956	Reinhardt	LP: Eurodisc OK 25290
Salzburg August 1965	Giesen	LP: Acanta 40.23529 CD: Acanta 43.529
Hannover March 1966	Giesen	CD: Bella voce 107.003 CD: Myto MCD 93278
Edinburgh September 1966	Giesen	Unpublished radio broadcast

Resignation (Lisch aus, mein Licht, was dir gebricht!)

Schwetzingen May 1965	Giesen	Unpublished radio broadcast
Salzburg August 1965	Giesen	LP: Acanta 40.23529 CD: Acanta 43.529
Munich October- November 1965	Giesen	LP: DG LPEM 39 125/SLPEM 139 125/ 2535 614/413 8371 CD: DG 429 9332/435 1452/447 9212
Hannover March 1966	Giesen	CD: Bella voce BV 107.003 CD: Myto MCD 93278
Edinburgh September 1966	Giesen	Unpublished radio broadcast

180   Wunderlich

Der Wachtelschlag (Horch, wie schallt's dorten so lieblich hervor!)

Salzburg August 1965	Giesen	LP: Acanta 40.23529 CD: Acanta 43.529
Hannover March 1966	Giesen	CD: Myto MCD 93278
Edinburgh September 1966	Giesen	Unpublished radio broadcast

Zärtliche Liebe (Ich liebe dich, so wie du mich)

Mainz November 1962	Reinhardt	Unpublished radio broadcast
Munich October- November 1965	Giesen	LP: DG LPEM 39 125/SLPEM 139 125 135 014/2535 614/2721 230/419 8371 CD: DG 429 9332/431 1102/435 1452/447 9212

Christus am Oelberge

Hilversum March 1957	Spoorenberg, Schey Hilversum Radio Orchestra & Chorus Spruit	CD: Bella voce 107.003

Fidelio: Excerpt (O welche Lust, in freier Luft den Atem leicht zu heben!)

Stuttgart November 1957	Role of First prisoner Nöcker SDR Orchestra and Chorus Rischner	LP: Acanta 23.568 CD: Acanta 43.267

Missa Solemnis

Berlin February 1966	Janowitz, C.Ludwig, Berry Wiener Singverein BPO Karajan	LP: DG KL 95-96/SKL 95-96/2707 030/ 2720 013/2721 135/2726 048/410 5351 CD: DG 423 9132 <u>Sanctus</u> LP: DG 2535 654/2563 632
Berlin February 1966	Janowitz, C.Ludwig, Berry Wiener Singverein BPO Karajan	CD: Hunt CDKAR 214

Symphony No 9 "Choral"

Stuttgart July 1955	Wachmann, Bence, Rohr Stuttgart PO Grischkat-Singkreis Diesenhaus	LP: Intercord 99309
Vienna June 1960	Lipp, Boese, Crass Wiener Singverein Philharmonia Klemperer	CD: Cetra CDE 1051 CD: Hunt CDGI 759 CD: Stradivarius STR 10003 CD: Grandi della classica 93.5121 CD: Music and Arts CD 886
Vienna October 1962	Stadler, Rössel-Majdan, Wächter Wiener Singverein VSO Böhm	Unpublished radio broadcast
Salzburg August 1965	Lorengar, Ahlin, Berry Wiener Singverein VPO Böhm	Unpublished radio broadcast

VINCENZO BELLINI (1801-1835)

La sonnambula, Excerpt (Prendi l'anel ti dono)

Munich January 1963	Köth Munich RO Eichhorn <u>Sung in German</u>	LP: DG 2535 801/413 8371 CD: DG 435 1452

182 Wunderlich

RALPH BENATZKY (1884-1957)

Ich muss wieder einmal in Grinzing sein

Munich August 1966	Spilar-Schrammeln	LP: Polydor Special 109 616-109 618 LP: Heliodor (USA) H 25051/HS 25051 LP: DG 413 8371 CD: DG 435 1452

Ich weiss auf der Wieden ein kleines Hotel

Vienna June 1966	Volksoper Orchestra Vienna Opera Chorus Stolz	LP: Polydor Special 109 616-109 618 LP: Heliodor (USA) H 25051/HS 25051 LP: DG 413 8371 CD: DG 435 1452

ALBAN BERG (1885-1935)

Wozzeck

Stuttgart November 1956	<u>Role of Andres</u> Kinas, Plümacher, Seider, Stolze, Blankenheim Württembergisches Staatsorcheser and Chorus Leitner	Unpublished radio broadcast

Berlin
March-
April 1965
	Lear, Oelke,
	Melchert, Stolze,
	Fischer-Dieskau
	Deutsche Oper
	Orchestra & Chorus
	Böhm
		LP: DG LPM 18 991-18 992/
		    SLPM 138 991-138 992/2709 023/
		    413 7979/413 8041
		CD: DG 435 7052

HANS BERNER

Carissima mia, sag' ja!

Freiburg October 1955	Südwestfunk Orchestra Stech	Unpublished radio broadcast

CESARE BIXIO

Sprich zu mir von Liebe

Kaiserslautern May 1958	Südwestfunk Orchestra Smola	Unpublished radio broadcast

GEORGES BIZET (1838-1875)

Les pêcheurs de perles, Excerpt (Au fond du temple saint)

Munich January 1963	Prey Munich RO Stein <u>Sung in German</u>	LP: DG 2535 801/2535 831/413 8371 CD: DG 435 1452

ERICH BOERSCHEL

Lass mich niemals mehr allein

Freiburg October 1955	Südwestfunk Orchestra Stech	Unpublished radio broadcast

CARL BOHM (1844-1920)

Still wie die Nacht

Munich May-June 1965	Graunke SO Carste	LP: Karussell 237 448/2435 198/2489 044 LP: Heliodor (USA) H 25063/HS 25063 LP: Polydor Special 109 616-109 618

FRANCOIS BOIELDIEU (1775-1834)

La dame blance, Excerpt (Viens, gentille dame!)

| Munich
November 1962 | Bavarian State
Orchestra
Müller-Kray
Sung in German | LP: Electrola E 80769/STE 80769
LP: EMI 1C 063 28420/EX 29 09883
LP: Angel 6157
CD: EMI CZS 762 9932 |

JOHANNES BRAHMS (1833-1897)

Deutsche Volkslieder: Es wohnet ein Fiedler zu Frankfurt-am-Main; Feinsliebchen, du sollst mir nicht barfuss geh'n; Des Abends kann ich nicht schlafen geh'n

| Mainz
November 1955 | Müller-Mayen | Unpublished radio broadcast |

Minnelied (Holder klingt der Vogelsang)

| Stuttgart
1956 | Reinhardt | LP: Eurodisc OK 25290/300 356.435/
301 185.370 |

Die Nachtigall/Volkskinderlied (Sitzt a schönes Vogerl aufm Dannabaum)

| Mainz
November 1955 | Müller-Mayen | Unpublished radio broadcast |

O liebliche Wangen, ihr macht mir Verlangen!

| Stuttgart
1956 | Reinhardt | LP: Eurodisc OK 25290/300 356.435/
301 185.370 |

Die Trennung (Da unten im Tale läuft's Wasser so trüb)

| Mainz
November 1955 | Müller-Mayen | Unpublished radio broadcast |

FRANZ JOSEF BREUER

Euch grüsst die Heimat

Munich May-June 1965	Lamy Choir Graunke SO Carste	45: Polydor 54 076

NICHOLAS BRODSZKY

Be my love (The Toast of New Orleans)

Munich May-June 1965	Lamy Choir Graunke SO Carste	LP: Karussell 237 448/2435 108/2489 044 LP: Heliodor (USA) H 25063/HS 25063 LP: Polydor Special 109 616-109 618

ANTON BRUCKNER (1824-1896)

Te Deum

Salzburg August 1960	L.Price, Rössel-Majdan, Berry Wiener Singverein VPO Karajan	Unpublished radio broadcast

HANS BUSCH

Viele schöne Tage

Freiburg February 1956	Südwestfunk Orchestra Stech	Unpublished radio broadcast

DIETRICH BUXTEHUDE (1637-1707)

O wie selig sind, die zu dem Abendmahl

Stuttgart March 1957	Werdermann Instrumentalists	Unpublished radio broadcast

Surrexit Christus hodie

Stuttgart March 1957	Guilleaume, Winkler Instrumentalists	Unpublished radio broadcast

Wachet auf, ruft uns die Stimme!

Stuttgart December 1956	H.Münch, Werdermann Instrumentalists	Unpublished radio broadcast

EDUARDO DI CAPUA

O sole mio (Che bella cosa)

Berlin 1957	Film orchestra Becker	LP: Eurodisc 300 356.435/301 188.370 CD: Eurodisc GD 69018
Munich January 1965	Graunke SO Carste	LP: Karussell 2562 040 LP: Polydor Special 109 616-109 618 LP: DG 2721 230/413 8371 CD: DG 435 1452 <u>This version has verses sung in Italian and German</u>

LUIGI CHERUBINI (1760-1842)

Les deux journées

Stuttgart November 1962	Role of Armand Hillebrecht, Cordes, Messthaler SDR Orchestra and Chorus Müller-Kray Sung in German	CD: Melodram CDM 19507 Excerpts CD: Verona 28044-28045

CARL CLEWING

Alle Tage ist kein Sonntag

Berlin 1957	Berlin SO Becker	LP: Karussell 2652 061 LP: Eurodisc 300 356.435/96 513 CD: Eurodisc GD 69018 CD: Munich Records MR 30007

LARRY COLEMAN

Walzer der Liebe

Freiburg March 1954	Südwestfunk Orchestra Stech	Unpublished radio broadcast

188 Wunderlich

PETER CORNELIUS (1824-1874)

Der Barbier von Bagdad, Excerpt (Vor deinem Fenster die Blumen)

Munich	Bavarian State	LP: Electrola E 80769/STE 80769
November 1962	Orchestra	LP: EMI 1C 063 28420
	Müller-Kray	CD: EMI CZS 762 9932

Der Barbier von Bagdad, Excerpt (Mein Sohn, sei Allahs Frieden hier auf Erden)

Stuttgart	Böhme	LP: Acanta 23.568
July 1957	SDR Orchestra	CD: Acanta 43.267
	Müller-Kray	

3 Kön'ge wandern aus Morgenland/Weihnachtslieder

Munich	Chorus	LP: Europäischer Fonoklub 63913
1957	Stadlmair	LP: Eurodisc XAU 47857/XB 25334/XC 85295

TEODORO COTTRAU (1827-1879)

Santa Lucia

Munich	Graunke SO	LP: Karussell 2430 254/2562 040
January 1965	Carste	LP: Polydor Special 109 616-109 618
	<u>Sung in German</u>	LP: DG 2721 230

ERNESTO DE CURTIS (1875-1937)

Non ti scordar di me

Berlin 1957	Berlin SO Becker Sung in German	CD: Eurodisc GD 69018 CD: Munich Records MR 30007
Munich January 1965	Graunke SO Carste Sung in German	LP: Karussell 2430 254 LP: Polydor Special 109 616-109 618 LP: DG 2721 230/413 8371
Munich February 1966	Munich RO Köhler Sung in German	Unpublished radio broadcast
Berlin February 1966	RIAS-Unterhaltungs- Orchester Carste Sung in German	Unpublished video recording

LUIGI DENZA

Funiculi funicula

Munich January 1965	Lamy Choir Graunke SO Carste	LP: Karussell 2562 040 LP: Polydor Special 109 616-109 618 LP: DG 2721 230/413 8371 CD: DG 431 1102/435 1452

GAETONO DONIZETTI (1797-1848)

Don Pasquale

Munich February 1961	Role of Ernesto Köth, Böhme Bavarian State Orchestra & Chorus Erede Sung in German	Unpublished video recording

Wunderlich

L'elisir d'amore, Excerpt (Una furtiva lagrima)

Berlin 1958	Berlin SO Kraus Sung in German	LP: Eurodisc XAK 85844/300 356.435/ 300 642.370/301 185.370/96 513
Munich November 1962	Bavarian State Orchestra Müller-Kray Sung in German	LP: Electrola E 80769/STE 80769 LP: EMI 1C 063 28420/EX 29 09883 LP: Angel 6157 CD: EMI CDC 747 6852
Munich December 1963	Munich RO Stein Sung in German	Unpublished radio broadcast

L'elisir d'amore, Excerpt (Quanto è bella!)

Munich November 1962	Bavarian State Orchestra Müller-Kray Sung in German	LP: Electrola E 80769/STE 80769 LP: EMI 1C 063 28420 CD: EMI CZS 762 9932

NICO DOSTAL (1895-1981)

Extrablätter, Excerpts (Wie tanzen dort die Paare; Es ist doch äusserst interessant)

Kaiserslautern July 1955	Assmann Südwestfunk Orchestra Smola	Unpublished radio broadcast

Der Kurier der Königin, Excerpt (Ihr schönen Frau'n, wer kann an Euch vorübergeh'n?)

Freiburg September 1956	Südwestfunk Orchestra Stech	Unpublished radio broadcast

Monika, Excerpt (Ein Walzer zu zweien)

Stuttgart 1957	Sailer Stuttgart PO Mareczek	LP: Vox STGBY 632 CD: ZYX Music CLS 42012

ANTONIN DVORAK (1841-1904)

Humoresque

Munich January 1965	Graunke SO Carste Sung in German	LP: Karussell 237 448/2435 108/2489 044 LP: Heliodor (USA) H 25063/HS 25063 LP: Polydor Special 109 616-109 618

WERNER EGK (1901-1983)

Columbus

Munich January- October 1963	Role of Ferdinand Montoya, Gutstein Bavarian Radio Orchestra & Chorus Egk	Unpublished radio broadcast and video recording

Furchtlosigkeit und Wohlwollen, cantata

Munich January 1960	Bavarian Radio Orchestra & Chorus Kertesz	Unpublished radio broadcast

Der Revisor

Schwetzingen May 1957 (9 May)	Role of Bobshinsky Sailer, Plümacher, Stolze, Ollendorff SDR Orchestra Egk	Unpublished radio broadcast Premiere performance
Schwetzingen May 1957 (28 May)	Sailer, Plümacher, Stolze, Ollendorff SDR Orchestra Egk	Unpublished video recording
Munich January 1960	Sailer, Plümacher, Stolze, Ollendorff Bavarian RO Egk	Unpublished radio broadcast

Die Verlobung in San Domingo

Munich November 1963	<u>Role of Christoph</u> Lear, Bence, Nöcker, Kohn, Yahia Bavarian State Orchestra Egk	CD: Orfeo C343 932I <u>Premiere performance</u>

Die Verlobung in San Domingo, Rehearsal extract and interview

Munich November 1963	Rennert	Unpublished video recording

RALPH ERWIN

Ich küsse Ihre Hand, Madame

Kaiserslautern November 1963	Südwestfunk Orchestra Smola	Unpublished radio broadcast
Munich May-June 1965	Graunke SO Carste	LP: Karussell 2435 108 LP: Heliodor (USA) H 25063/HS 25063 LP: Polydor Special 109 616-109 618

LEO FALL (1873-1925)

Der fidele Bauer, Querschnitt

Munich September 1963	Knittel, Fassbaender, Hoppe, Kusche Lamy Choir Graunke SO Michalski	LP: Columbia (Germany) SMC 83456 LP: EMI 1C 061 28189 CD: Kaiserliche Operette 863.532 <u>Frag mich nicht, mein süsser Schatz</u> LP: EMI 1C 061 28064/HQS 1168/ EX 29 09883 LP: Angel 6157 CD: EMI CZS 762 9932

Die Rose von Stambul

Cologne May 1962	Role of Achmed Bey Bartos, Hartung, Hänsler WDR Orchestra and Chorus Marszalek	Unpublished radio broadcast Excerpts LP: RCA VL 30318/VL 30407 CD: Sonia 74505

Die Rose von Stambul, Querschnitt

Munich September 1963	Muszely, Friedauer Graunke SO Michalski	LP: Columbia (Germany) C 83454/SMC 83454 LP: EMI 1C 061 28187 CD: Kaiserliche Operette 863 532 Excerpts LP: EMI 1C 061 28064/1C 061 28163 LP: EMI HQS 1253/SHZE 193/EX 29 09883 LP: Angel 6157/60043 CD: EMI CZS 762 9932

Die Rose von Stambul, Excerpt (O Rose von Stambul)

Munich June 1962	Munich RO Moltkau	Unpublished radio broadcast
Munich November 1962	Bavarian RO Moltkau	LP: Electrola E 80768/STE 80768/SME 83691 LP: EMI 1C 061 28064/1C 061 28163/ HQS 1168/EX 29 09883 CD: EMI CZS 762 9932

Die Rose von Stambul, Excerpt (Zwei Augen, die wollen mir nicht aus dem Sinn)

Munich June 1962	Munich RO	Unpublished radio broadcast
Munich November 1962	Bavarian State Orchestra Moltkau	LP: Electrola E 80768/STE 80768 LP: EMI 1C 061 28163/HQS 1253 CD: EMI CZS 762 9932

HEINRICH FEISCHNER

Zirkus Carambas, opera

Stuttgart February 1957- April 1958	Role of Silvio Paul, Litz, Günter, Kusche SDR Orchestra and Chorus Müller-Kray	Unpublished radio broadcast

HEINRICH FINCK (1445-1527)

O schönstes Weib

Berlin January 1962	Instrumentalists	LP: Columbia (Germany) C 91107/SMC 91107 LP: EMI 1C 037 46523 LP: Angel 36379 CD: EMI CZS 252 3852/CZS 252 2382

FRIEDRICH VON FLOTOW (1812-1883)

Martha, Querschnitt

Berlin May 1960	Role of Lyonel Rothenberger, Plümacher, Frick, G.Völker Berlin SO Deutsche Oper Chorus Klobucar	LP: Odeon O 80593/STO 80593 LP: HMV CLP 1679/CSD 1511 LP: Angel 36236 LP: EMI 1C 037 30713 CD: EMI CDZ 252 2152/CZS 253 0472 Excerpts 45: Electrola E 41543/SME 41543 LP: Electrola E 80847/SME 80847 LP: EMI 1C 063 28173/SHZE 193/ HQS 1168/EX 29 09883 LP: Angel 6157/60043 CD: EMI CZS 762 9932

Martha, Excerpt (Ach so fromm)

Berlin 1958	Berlin SO Rother	LP: Eurodisc KR 70259/OU 27037/ XA 25289/XB 86838/300 356.435/ 301 188.370/96 513

NELSON FREIRE (born 1944)

Sleep, little blonde angel

Munich	Graunke SO	LP: Karussell 247 448/535 009/2489 044
May-June	Carste	LP: Polydor Special 109 616-109 618
1965	Sung in German	

ADAM VON FULDA (1445-1505)

Apollo aller Kunst

Mainz	Instrumentalists	Unpublished radio broadcast
Date uncertain		

GUENTER GEORGY-ENGELHARDT

Gondel, gleite du hinaus!

Freiburg	Südwestfunk	Unpublished radio broadcast
September 1956	Orchestra	
	Stech	

Wunderlich

JEAN GILBERT (1879-1941)

Die keusche Susanna, Excerpts (Wenn die Füsschen sich heben; Wer kann dafür?)

Kaiserslautern	Wachmann	Unpublished radio broadcast
January 1957	Südwestfunk	
	Orchestra	
	Smola	

Uschi, Excerpt (Liebe und Glück, kehr nicht mehr zurück!)

Kaiserslautern	Wachmann	Unpublished radio broadcast
January 1957	Südwestfunk	
	Orchestra	
	Smola	

Das Weib in Purpur, Excerpts (Mädels gibt's auf der Welt; Niemals kann Liebe ganz vergeh'n)

Kaiserslautern	Wachmann	Unpublished radio broadcast
January 1957	Südwestfunk	
	Orchestra	
	Smola	

TOMMASO GIORDANI (1730-1806)

Caro mio ben

Berlin 1957	Berlin SO Becker	LP: Eurodisc OE 88952/OU 27037/XB 28403/ 300 356.435/301 185.370/96 513 CD: Eurodisc GD 69018 CD: Munich Records MR 30007
Munich May-June 1965	Graunke SO Carste	LP: Karussell 237 448/2435 108/2489 044 LP: Heliodor (USA) H 25063/HS 25063 LP: Polydor Special 109 616-109 618

CHRISTOPH WILLIBALD GLUCK (1714-1787)

Iphigenie auf Tauris

Munich March 1965	Role of Pylades Jurinac, Fahberg, Engen, Prey Bavarian Radio Orchestra & Chorus Kubelik	CD: Myto MCD 91544 Excerpts LP: DG 2535 831/2700 709/413 8371 CD: DG 435 1452 CD: Verona 28044-28045

Die gerechtfertigte Unschuld, Excerpt (Alte Eichen an schwindelnden Hängen)

Kaiserslautern January 1959	Südwestfunk- Unterhaltungs- Orchester Smola	Unpublished radio broadcast

CHARLES GOUNOD (1818-1893)

Ave Maria

Munich January 1965	Lamy Choir Graunke SO Carste Sung in German	LP: Karussell 2430 254/2562 040 LP: Polydor Special 109 616-109 618

ALESSANDRO GRANDI (1577-1630)

Plorabo die ac nocte

Stuttgart March 1957	Guilleaume, Winkler, Werdermann Instrumentalists	Unpublished radio broadcast

JOHANN CHRISTIAN GRAUPNER (1683-1760)

Wie bald hast du gelitten

Stuttgart February 1956	Guilleaume, H.Münch, Werdermann Instrumentalists	Unpublished radio broadcast

FRANZ GROTHE (1908-1982)

Kleine Melodie

Freiburg March 1954	Südwestfunk Orchestra Stech	Unpublished radio broadcast

Mon bijou

Freiburg September 1956	Südwestfunk Orchestra Stech	Unpublished radio broadcast

Serenade der Nacht

Freiburg March 1954	Südwestfunk Orchestra Stech	Unpublished radio broadcast

PAUL GRUA (1754-1833)

Dulcis Jesu

Rohr May 1962	Collegium musicum Regensburg Schwarzmaier	Unpublished radio broadcast

GEORGE FRIDERIC HANDEL (1685-1759)

Alcina

Cologne May 1959	Role of Ruggiero Sutherland, Van Dijck, Procter, Monti, Hemsley WDR Chorus Capella coloniensis Leitner Performed in Italian but with German dialogue	CD: Melodram CDM 37002 CD: Verona 27011-27013 CD: Rodolphe RPC 32563-32564 Excerpts CD: Myto MCD 91752

Jephta

Freiburg June 1961	Role of Jephta Sailer, Naaff, R.Hermann South-West German Chamber Orchestra and Chorus Ummenhofer Sung in German	Unpublished radio broadcast

Judas Maccabaeus

Munich October 1963	Role of Maccabaeus Giebel, Falk, Pöld, Welter Bavarian Radio Orchestra & Chorus Kubelik Sung in German	LP: Movimento musica 02.025 CD: Melodram MEL 28026 Excerpts CD: Verona 28044-28045

Julius Caesar

Munich July 1965	Role of Sextus Popp, C.Ludwig, Berry, Kohn, Nöcker Bavarian Radio Chorus Munich PO Leitner Sung in German	CD: Melodram CDM 37059 CD: Orfeo C351 943D Excerpt LP: DG 2535 831/413 8371 Melodram incorrectly dated March 1966

Messiah

Stuttgart March 1959	Briem, Bence, Rohr Stuttgart Philharmonic Choir SDR Orchestra Mende Sung in German	CD: Myto MCD 92571 Excerpts LP: Acanta 23.586 CD: Melodram CDM 28026 CD: Verona 28044-28045

Serse

Munich October 1962	Role of Serse Hallstein, Töpper, Pöld, Cook, Kohn, Proebstl Bavarian Radio Orchestra & Chorus Kubelik Sung in German	CD: Verona 27032-27033 Excerpts LP: DG 2535 831/2700 709/413 8371 CD: DG 435 1452 CD: Melodram CDM 28026 CD: Myto MCD 91752

Serse, Excerpt (Ombra mai fù)

Berlin 1957	Berlin SO Becker	LP: Eurodisc OE 88952/OU 27037/XB 25334/ XB 28403/300 356.435/301 185.370 CD: Eurodisc GD 69018/610.230
Stuttgart March 1959	SDR Orchestra Rischner	LP: Acanta 23.568
Munich November 1962	Bavarian State Orchestra Müller-Kray	45: Electrola E 41543/SME 41543 LP: Electrola E 80769/SME 80759 LP: EMI 1C 063 28420/1C 061 28801/ 1C 037 30954/HQS 1168 CD: EMI CZS 762 9932

HANNO HANSON

Mutterlied (Die Zeit der Kindheit geht so schnell dahin)

Freiburg July 1957	Südwestfunk Orchestra Stech	Unpublished radio broadcast

KURT HASENPFLUG

Von Liebe und von Glück

Freiburg October 1955	Südwestfunk Orchestra Stech	Unpublished radio broadcast

FRANZ JOSEF HAYDN (1732-1809)

Die Jahreszeiten

Schwetzingen May 1959	Giebel, Engen SDR Orchestra and Chorus Müller-Kray	CD: Bella voce BLV 107.204 Excerpts LP: Acanta 23.568

Mass No 10 "Missa in tempore belli"

Salzburg August 1959	Dutoit, Pitzinger, Pacher Salzburger Domchor Mozarteum Orchestra Messner	Unpublished radio broadcast

Mass No 12 "Theresienmesse"

Rohr May 1962	Schädle, Benningsen, Engen Regensburg Collegium musicum and Chorus Schwarzmaier	Unpublished radio broadcast

Die Schöpfung

Hilversum March 1958	Schädle, Schey Hilversum Radio Orchestra & Chorus Haitink	Unpublished radio broadcast
Salzburg August 1965	Janowitz, Borg, Prey Vienna Singverein VPO Karajan	CD: Hunt CDKAR 203 Excerpts CD: Bella voce BLV 107.204
Berlin February 1966	Arias only Janowitz, C.Ludwig, Krenn (tenor recitatives), Fischer-Dieskau, Berry Wiener Singverein BPO Karajan	LP: DG 643 515-643 516/2707 044/410 9511 CD: DG 435 0772 Excerpts LP: DG 136 439/2535 146/2535 609/ 2545 055/2563 632 CD: DG 439 4542

Schottische Lieder: Es weiden meine Schafe; Mein süsses Liebchen, schläfst du noch?; Fliess' leise, mein Bächlein

Vienna May 1963	H.Schmidt Weller, violin Beinl, cello	LP: Philips 6520 022 CD: Philips 420 8522

Walisische Lieder: Ein Wanderer kommt von ferne; Rose rot, Rose weiss, wie süss ist doch dein Mund; Ich stehe auf der Heide; Im Schlummer

Vienna May 1963	H.Schmidt Weller, violin Beinl, cello	LP: Philips 6520 022 CD: Philips 420 8522

CARL HEINS

Zwei dunkle Augen

Berlin	FFB-Orchester	LP: Electrola SHZE 193
January 1962	Eisbrenner	LP: Angel 60043
		CD: EMI CZS 762 9932

EVERETT HELM (born 1913)

The Siege of Tottenburg

Stuttgart	<u>Role of Lieutenant</u>	Unpublished radio broadcast
May 1956	Plümacher,	
	Fehringer, Günter,	
	Ambrosius	
	SDR Orchestra	
	and Chorus	
	Müller-Kray	
	<u>Sung in German</u>	

GEORG HILLER

Du sollst nicht traurig sein

Kaiserslautern	Südwestfunk	Unpublished radio broadcast
June 1954	Orchestra	
	Smola	

PAUL HOFHAIMER (1459-1537)

Was ich durch Glück

Mainz	Instrumentalists	Unpublished radio broadcast
Date uncertain		

IGNAZ HOLZBAUER (1711-1783)

Günther von Schwarzburg, Excerpts (Schönster Sohn des Himmels, holder Frieden; Umfing ich deine Hand)

Kaiserslautern April 1959	Verlooy Südwestfunk- Unterhaltungs- Orchester Smola	Unpublished radio broadcast

HANS GEORG HUEBSCH (1910-1990)

Herr Hofrat, erinnern Sie sich noch?

Munich August 1966	Spilar-Schrammeln	LP: Polydor Special 109 616-109 618 LP: Karussell 2415 030

TIBOR INCZEDY

Glückswalzer (Sag' nie, es ist zu spät für's grosse Glück)

Freiburg February 1955	Südwestfunk Orchestra Stech	Unpublished radio broadcast

Das Lied der Liebe sing' ich dir allein

Freiburg May 1955	Südwestfunk Orchestra Stech	Unpublished radio broadcast

HEINRICH IZAAK (1450-1517)

Ach weiblich Art

Mainz Date uncertain	Instrumentalists	Unpublished radio broadcast

Mein Freund allein

Berlin January 1962	Instrumentalists	LP: Columbia (Germany) C 91107/SMC 91107 LP: Angel 36379 LP: EMI 1C 037 46523 CD: EMI CZS 252 3852/CZS 252 2382

WALTER JAEGER

Mädele

Freiburg December 1953	Südwestfunk Orchestra Stech	Unpublished radio broadcast

LEOS JANACEK (1854-1928)

The Excursions of Mr Broucek

Cologne September 1959	<u>Role of Mazal</u> Lipp, Fahberg, Benningsen, Fehenberger, Kuen, Alexander WDR Orchestra and Chorus Keilberth <u>Sung in German</u>	Unpublished radio broadcast
Munich November 1959	Lipp, Fahberg, Benningsen, Fehenberger, Kuen. Böhme Bavarian State Orchestra & Chorus Keilberth <u>Sung in German</u>	CD: Orfeo C354 942I <u>Excerpts</u> CD: Verona 28044-28045 <u>German stage premiere; excerpts CD</u> <u>incorrectly describes the work as</u> <u>Cunning Little Vixen</u>

Fate

Stuttgart October 1958	<u>Role of Singer</u> Bauer, Bence, Wissmann, Traxel, Nöcker Württemberg State Orchestra Schwieger <u>Sung in German</u>	Unpublished radio broadcast

EMIL KAISER

Veilchen, Liebe, Frühling und Du

Freiburg December 1953	Südwestfunk Orchestra Stech	Unpublished radio broadcast

CHARLES KALMAN (born 1929)

Wir reisen um die Welt, Excerpts (Du allein schenkst mir das Leben; Ich träume nur von Liebe; Wann kommt die eine, die ich liebe?)

Kaiserslautern July 1955	Assmann Südwestfunk Orchestra Smola	Unpublished radio broadcast

EMMERICH KALMAN (1882-1953)

Arizona Lady, Excerpt (Kleiner Cowboy)

Freiburg February 1956	Südwestfunk- Unterhaltungs- Orchester Stech <u>Wunderlich also plays trumpet solo in this recording</u>	Unpublished radio broadcast

Die Csardasfürstin, Querschnitt

Cologne January 1959	<u>Role of Edwin</u> Holm, Talmar, W,Hofmann, Kusche WDR Orchestra and Chorus Marszalek	45: Polydor 20 091/21 419 LP: Polydor 237 158

Gräfin Maritza

Cologne October 1963	<u>Role of Tassilo</u> Hartung, Görner, W.Hofmann, Kusche WDR Orchestra and Chorus Marszalek	Unpublished radio broadcast <u>Abridged version</u> LP: RCA VL 30315 CD: Sonia 74505

Gräfin Maritza, Excerpt (Grüss' mir mein Wien)

Munich November 1962	Bavarian State Orchestra Moltkau	LP: Electrola E 80768/STE 80768/SME 83691 LP: EMI 1C 061 28163/HQS 1253/EX 29 09883 LP: Angel 6157 CD: EMI CZS 762 9932
Freiburg November 1963	Südwestfunk- Unterhaltungs- Orchester Mattes	Unpublished radio broadcast
Vienna June 1966	Volksoper Orchestra Stolz	DG unpublished

Gräfin Maritza, Excerpt (Komm Zigany!)

Munich November 1962	Bavarian State Orchestra Moltkau	LP: Electrola E 80768/STE 80768/SME 83691 LP: EMI 1C 061 28163/HQS 1168/EX 29 09883 LP: Angel 6157 CD: EMI CZS 762 9932

Kaiserin Josephine, Excerpts (Du bist die Frau, die mein Herz; Liebe singt ihr Zauberlied; Schön ist der Tag)

Stuttgart February 1958	Hennig Südwestfunk- Unterhaltungs- Orchester Marszalek	Unpublished radio broadcast

Die Zirkusprinzessin, Excerpt (Zwei Märchenaugen, wie die Sterne schön)

Berlin 1957	Berlin SO Melichar	LP: Europäischer Fonoklub 3170 LP: Eurodisc IE 70347/OE 88946/XN 87794/ 300 356.435/301 188.370 LP: Maritim FU 47093 CD: Eurodisc GD 69018 CD: Munich Records MR 30007

Munich
November 1962
	Bavarian State
	Orchestra
	Moltkau
		LP: Electrola E 80768/STE 80768/
		    SME 83691/SHZE 193
		LP: EMI 1C 061 28163/HQS 1168 /EX 29 09883/
		    1C 187 30179-30189
		LP: Angel 6157/60043
		CD: EMI CDC 747 6852

EDMUND KASPER

Bella Maria

Freiburg February 1955	Südwestfunk Orchestra Stech	Unpublished radio broadcast

MAURUS KATT

Wenn mein Herz Heimweh hat

Freiburg February 1957	Südwestfunk Orchestra Stech	Unpublished radio broadcast

RUDOLF KATTNIGG

Man sagt sich du

Freiburg September 1956	Südwestfunk Orchestra Stech	Unpublished radio broadcast

WILHELM KIENZL (1857-1941)

Der Evangelimann, Excerpt (Selig sind, die Verfolgung leiden)

Berlin 1958	Schönberger Sängerknaben Berlin SO Rother	LP: Eurodisc KR 70259/XA 25289/XB 28403/ 300 356.435/301 188.370/96 513
Munich November 1962	Kinderkreis St.Wolfgang Bavarian State Orchestra Müller-Kray	45: Electrola E 41543/SME 41543 LP: Electrola E 80769/STE 80769 LP: EMI 1C 063 28420 CD: EMI CZS 762 9932

Der Kuhreigen, Excerpt (Zu Strassburg auf der Schanz)

Stuttgart March 1959	SDR Orchestra and Chorus Rischner	LP: Acanta 23.568 CD: Acanta 43.267

LEO KOWALSKI

Singende Gitarre

Freiburg May 1955	Stingl Südwestfunk Orchestra Stech	Unpublished radio broadcast

CONRADIN KREUTZER (1780-1849)

Das Nachtlager von Granada, Excerpt (Trenne nicht das Band der Liebe)

Munich December 1961	Köth, Prey Munich RO Eichhorn	Unpublished radio broadcast
Munich September 1962	Köth, Prey Munich RO Eichhorn	LP: DG 2535 831/2700 709/413 8371 CD: DG 435 1452

ADAM KRIEGER (1634-1666)

Amanda, darf man dich wohl küssen?

Berlin January 1962	Instrumentalists	LP: Columbia (Germany) C 91111/SMC 91111 LP: EMI 1C 037 45576 CD: EMI CDZ 252 3872

JOHANN PHILIP KRIEGER (1649-1725)

Wo willst du hin, weil's Abend ist?

Untertürkheim March 1956	Michaelis Instrumentalists	Unpublished radio broadcast

HERMANN KROME (1888-1955)

Sonne über Capri; Uebers Meer grüss' ich dich

Freiburg February 1957	Südwestfunk Orchestra Stech	Unpublished radio broadcast

EDUARD KUENNEKE (1885-1953)

Die grosse Sünderin, Excerpt (Das Lied vom Leben des Schrenk)

Munich June 1962	Munich RO Moltkau	Unpublished radio broadcast
Munich November 1962	Bavarian State Orchestra Moltkau	LP: Electrola E 80768/STE 80768/SME 83691 LP: EMI 1C 061 28163/HQS 1253/EX 29 09883 LP: Angel 6157 CD: EMI CD 747 6852

Die lockende Flamme, Excerpt (Ich träumte mit offenen Augen)

Munich June 1962	Munich RO Moltkau	Unpublished radio broadcast

Der Vetter aus Dingsda, Excerpt (Ich bin nur ein armer Wandergesell)

Berlin
1957
	Berlin SO
	Becker
		LP: Europäischer Fonoklub 44923
		LP: Eurodisc IE 70347/OE 88952/OE 88946/
		    XB 86838/XF 76499/XN 87794/XQ 27252/
		    300 356.435/301 188.370/96 513
		CD: Munich Records MR 30007

Zauberin Lola, Excerpt (Du warst von Anbeginn nur mir bestimmt)

Stuttgart 1957	Sailer Stuttgart PO Mareczek	LP: Vox STBGY 632

ERASMUS LAPICIDA

Es lebt mein Herz

Mainz Instrumentalists Unpublished radio broadcast
Date iuncertain

AUGUSTIN LARA (1900-1970)

Granada

Berlin   FFB-Orchester   CD: Eurodisc GD 69018
1957   Becker   CD: Munich Records MR 30007

Kaiserslautern   Südwestfunk   Unpublished radio broadcast
November 1965   Orchestra
                  Smola

Munich   Graunke SO   LP: Karussell 237 448/535 009/
May-June   Carste   2489 044/2562 040
1965   LP: Heliodor (USA) H 25063/HS 25063
                                       LP: Polydor Special 109 616-109 618
                                       LP: DG 2721 230/413 8371
                                       CD: DG 435 1452

SALZBURGER FESTSPIELE 1960

40 JAHRE SALZBURGER FESTSPIELE

DIE ZAUBERFLÖTE

OPER IN ZWEI AUFZÜGEN
TEXT VON EMANUEL SCHIKANEDER

MUSIK VON
WOLFGANG AMADEUS MOZART

DIRIGENT
JOSEPH KEILBERTH

INSZENIERUNG
GÜNTHER RENNERT

BÜHNENBILD UND KOSTÜME
ITA MAXIMOWNA

ORCHESTER
DIE WIENER PHILHARMONIKER
CHOR DER WIENER STAATSOPER

DIE ZAUBERFLÖTE

Oper in zwei Aufzügen
Text von Emanuel Schikaneder

MUSIK VON WOLFGANG AMADEUS MOZART

Sarastro	Gottlob Frick
Tamino	Fritz Wunderlich
Sprecher	Eberhard Wächter
Erster Priester	Erich Majkut
Zweiter Priester	Ljubomir Pantscheff
Königin der Nacht	Mimi Coertse
Pamina, ihre Tochter	Liselotte Fölser
Erste Dame	Lisa Otto
Zweite Dame	Hetty Plümacher
Dritte Dame	Sieglinde Wagner
Papageno	Walter Berry
Papagena	Graziella Sciutti
Monostatos, ein Mohr	Kurt Marschner
Erster Knabe	
Zweiter Knabe	Drei Wiener Sängerknaben
Dritter Knabe	
Erster Geharnischter	Robert Charlebois
Zweiter Geharnischter	Alois Pernerstorfer

Priester, Sklaven, Gefolge

Schlußbild des zweiten Aufzuges nach Oscar Strnad

Nach dem ersten Aufzug eine größere Pause

FRANZ LEHAR (1870-1948)

Friederike, Excerpt (O Mädchen, mein Mädchen!)

Berlin 1957	Berlin SO Melichar	LP: Europäischer Fonoklub 3170 LP: Eurodisc XF 77665/300 356.435/ 301 188.370/96 513 LP: Maritim FE 47017 CD: Eurodisc GD 69018/610 230

Giuditta, Excerpt (O Freunde, das Leben ist lebenswert!)

Berlin
1957
	Berlin SO
	Melichar
		LP: Europäischer Fonoklub 3170
		LP: Eurodisc OE 88946/OU 27037/XB 86838/
		    XF 76499/XF 77665/XN 87794/IE 70347/
		    300 356.435/301 188.370/96 513
		LP: Maritim FE 47017
		CD: Eurodisc GD 69018/610 230
		CD: Munich Records MR 30007

Munich June 1962	Munich RO Moltkau	Unpublished radio broadcast
Munich November 1962	Bavarian State Orchestra Moltkau	LP: Electrola E 80768/STE 80768/SME 83691 LP: EMI 1C 061 28163/HQS 1168/EX 29 09883 LP: Angel 6157 CD: EMI CZS 762 9932
Kaiserslautern November 1965	Südwestfunk Orchestra Smola	LP: RCA VL 30318/VL 30366 LP: Acanta 23.567 CD: Acanta 43.567 CD: Sonia 74 505

Das Land des Lächelns

Cologne January 1961	Role of Sou Chong Fahberg, Cramer, Peysang WDR Orchestra Marszalek	LP: RCA VL 30318 CD: Sonia 74505 Immer nur lächeln LP: Acanta 23.567 CD: Acanta 43.567 This recording of the operetta also used as playback for a TV recording

Das Land des Lächelns, Querschnitt

Munich September 1963- January 1964	Muszely, Görner, Friedauer Graunke SO Michalski	LP: Columbia (Germany) C 83455/SMC 83455 LP: EMI 1C 061 28188 CD: Laserlight 16046 Excerpts LP: EMI 1C 061 28064/1C 06328420/SHZE 193/ HQS 1168/HQS 1253/EX 29 09883 LP: Angel 6157/60043 CD: EMI CDC 747 6852/CZS 762 9932

Paganini, Excerpt (Niemand liebt dich so wie ich)

Munich February 1966	Pütz Munich RO Köhler	CD: Originals SH 866

Schön ist die Welt, Excerpt (Schön ist die Welt)

Berlin
1958
	Berlin SO
	Melichar
		LP: Europäischer Fonoklub 3170
		LP: Eurodisc IE 70347/OE 88946/XF 76499/
		    XF 77665/300 356.435/301 188.370/
		    96 513
		LP: Maritim FE 47017
		CD: Eurodisc GD 69018
		CD: Munich Records MR 30007
		<u>CD contains alternative arrangement
		of the aria recorded at the same time</u>

Munich June 1962	Munich RO Moltkau	Unpublished radio broadcast

Der Zarewitsch, Querschnitt

Munich September 1963- January 1964	<u>Role of Zarewitsch</u> Muszely, Görner, Hgara Lamy Choir Graunke SO Michalski	LP: Columbia (Germany) C 83455/SMC 83455 LP: EMI 1C 061 28188 Excerpts LP: EMI 1C 061 28064 CD: EMI CZS 762 9932

218 Wunderlich

Der Zarewitsch, Excerpt (Hab' nur dich allein)

Stuttgart	Sailer	LP: Vox STGBY 632
1957	Stuttgart PO	LP: Eurodisc XF 77665
	Mareczek	CD: Zyx Music CLS 42012

Der Zarewitsch, Excerpt (Allein wieder allein/Wolgalied)

Berlin	Berlin SO	LP: Europäischer Fonoklub 3170
1958	Melichar	LP: Karussell 2652 061
		LP: Eurodisc OE 88946/XF 77665/XQ 27252/ XN 87794/300 356.435/301 188.370/ IE 70347
		LP: Maritim FE 47017
		CD: Munich Records MR 30007
		CD: Eurodisc GD 69018/610 230
Munich November 1962	Bavarian State Orchestra Moltkau	LP: Electrola E 80768/STE 80768/SME 83691 LP: EMI 1C 061 28163/SHZE 193/HQS 1168/ 1C 148 31396-31399/EX 29 09883 LP: Angel 6157/60043 CD: EMI CDC 747 6852
Kaiserslautern November 1965	Südwestfunk Orchestra Smola	LP: Acanta 23.567 LP: RCA VL 30318 CD: Acanta 43.567 CD: Sonia 74505

RUGGIERO LEONCAVALLO (1857-1919)

Mattinata

Munich January 1965	Graunke SO Carste	LP: Karussell 535 009/2634 021 LP: Polydor Special 109 616-109 618 LP: DG 2721 230/413 8371 CD: DG 435 1452
Munich February 1966	Munich RO Köhler	CD: Originals SH 866

TONI LEUTWILER (born 1923)

Es gibt eine Zeit

Freiburg February 1957	Südwestfunk Orchestra Stech	Unpublished radio broadcast

Florentiner Mai

Freiburg February 1957	Südwestfunk Orchestra Stech	Unpublished radio broadcast

Narzissen aus Montreux

Freiburg July 1957	Südwestfunk Orchestra Stech	Unpublished radio broadcast

FRANZ LISZT (1811-1851)

Es muss ein Wunderbares sein

Berlin
1957
	Berlin SO
	Becker
		LP: Eurodisc OE 88952/200 606.250/
		    200 941.315/201 981.315/
		    300 356.435/301 188.370/96 513
		CD: Eurodisc GD 69018
		CD: Munich Records MR 30007

ALBERT LORTZING (1801-1851)

Undine, Excerpt (Ich ritt zum grossen Waffenspiele)

Kaiserslautern March 1957	Sailer Südwestfunk- Unterhaltungs- Orchester Smola	Unpublished radio broadcast

Undine, Excerpt (Vater, Mutter, Schwestern, Brüder!)

Stuttgart June 1957	SDR Orchestra Rischner	LP: Acanta 23.567 CD: Acanta 43.567
Berlin 1958	Berlin SO Rother	LP: XA 25289/XA 77831/XB 86838/KR 70259/ 300 356.435/301 188.370/96 513 CD: Eurodisc GD 69018/610 230
Munich December 1959	Munich RO Zallinger	Unpublished radio broadcast

Der Waffenschmied, Excerpt (Man wird ja einmal nur geboren)

Stuttgart June 1957	SDR Orchestra Rischner	LP: Acanta 23.567 CD: Acanta 43.567
Berlin 1958	Berlin SO Rother	LP: Eurodisc XA 25289/KR 70259/96 513/ 300 356.435/301 188.370
Munich March 1962	Munich RO Moltkau	LP: DG 2535 801/2700 709/2721 230/413 8371 CD: DG 431 1102/435 1452

Der Waffenschmied, Excerpt (War einst ein junger Springinsfeld)

Stuttgart June 1957	SDR Orchestra Rischner	LP: Acanta 23.567 CD: Acanta 43.567

Der Wildschütz

Munich
May 1963
	Role of Kronthal
	Rothenberger,
	Litz, Prey,
	Ollendorff
	Bavarian State
	Orchestra & Chorus
	Heger
		LP: Columbia (Germany) C 91287-91289/
		    STC 91287-91289
		LP: EMI 1C 163 28534-28536
		CD: EMI CMS 763 2052
		Excerpts
		LP: Electrola E 80847/SME 80847
		LP: EMI 1C 063 28173/1C 063 29004/
		    1C 187 29298-29299/EX 29 09883
		LP: Angel 6157
		CD: EMI CDZ 252 2192/CZS 253 0472
		    CZS 762 9932/CZS 252 3492

Zar und Zimmermann, Querschnitt

Berlin November 1959	Role of Chateauneuf Hildebrand, Cordes, Frick, Wiemann Berlin SO Deutsche Oper Chorus Klobucar	LP: Electrola WCLP 654/E 80568/STE 80568 LP: EMI 1C 047 28565 CD: EMI CDZ 252 2212/CZS 253 0472 Leb wohl, mein flandrisch' Mädchen LP: Electrola E 80847/SME 80847 LP: EMI 1C 063 28173/HQS 1253/EX 29 09883/ 1C 187 29298-29299 LP: Angel 6157
Bamberg September 1966	Hallstein, Kohn, Fischer-Dieskau Bavarian Radio Chorus Bamberg SO Gierster	LP: DG 136 432/2537 004 CD: DG 445 0472 Leb wohl, mein flandrisch' Mädchen LP: DG 2535 627/2562 040/2721 230/413 8371 CD: DG 431 1102/435 1452 CD Querschnitt contains an ensemble which was not on the original LP

Zar und Zimmermann, Excerpt (Leb wohl, mein flandrisch' Mädchen)

Munich April 1965	Bavarian Radio Chorus Munich RO Eichhorn	Unpublished radio broadcast

GUSTAV MAHLER (1860-1911)

Das Lied von der Erde

Bamberg April 1964	Fischer-Dieskau Bamberg SO Keilberth	Unpublished radio broadcast
Vienna June 1964	Fischer-Dieskau VSO Keilberth	Unpublished radio broadcast <u>According to Johann Gratz this performance is actually conducted by Josef Krips</u>
London November 1964	C.Ludwig Philharmonia Klemperer	LP: EMI AN 179/SAN 179/SMC 91639/ 1C 065 00065/EL 29 04401 LP: Angel 3704 CD: EMI CDC 747 2312
Hamburg April 1965	Merriman NDR Orchestra Schmidt-Isserstedt	Unpublished radio broadcast

Symphony No 8

Vienna June 1960	Muszely, Scheyrer, Lipp, Boese, Rössel-Majdan, Prey, Edelmann Wiener Singverein VSO Keilberth	Unpublished radio broadcast

LOUIS-AIME MAILLART (1817-1871)

Les dragons de Villars, Excerpt (Il m'aime, espoir charmant)

Munich May 1962	Munich RO Moltkau <u>Sung in German</u>	LP: DG 2535 831/413 8371 CD: DG 435 1452

FRANK MARTIN (1890-1974)

In terra pax

Freiburg November 1953	Giebel, Höffgen, Brauer Freiburg Bach Choir Freiburg PO Sandoz	Unpublished radio broadcast

JEAN PAUL MARTINI (1741-1816)

Plaisir d'amour

Munich May-June 1965	Graunke SO Carste	LP: Karussell 237 448/535 009/2489 044 LP: Heliodor (USA) H 25063/HS 25063 LP: Polydor Special 109 616-109 618 LP: Polydor 2634 021

PIETRO MASCAGNI (1863-1945)

Cavalleria rusticana, Querschnitt

Berlin 1956	Role of Turiddu Siemeling, Wenglor, Niese Arndt Choir Deutsche Oper Orchestra Sung in German	LP: Baccarola 75 877 Excerpts LP: Eurodisc KR 70259/XA 25289/ 300 356.435/301 185.370/96 513

JULES MASSENET (1842-1912)

Manon, Excerpt (En fermant les yeux)

Munich November 1962	Bavarian State Orchestra Müller-Kray Sung in German	LP: Electrola E 80769/STE 80769 LP: EMI 1C 063 28420/EX 29 09883 LP: Angel 6157 CD: EMI CZS 762 9932

WILLY MATTES (born 1916)

Deine Liebe ist mein ganzes Leben

Munich May 1962	Munich RO Mattes	Unpublished radio broadcast
Stuttgart November 1963	Südfunk- Unterhaltungs- Orchester Mattes	Unpublished radio broadcast

Melodia con passione (Tag für Tag seh' ich dich durch die Strassen geh'n)

Munich May 1962	Munich RO Mattes	Unpublished radio broadcast
Munich October 1963	Munich RO Mattes	Unpublished radio broadcast
Stuttgart November 1963	Südfunk- Unterhaltungs- Orchester Mattes	Unpublished radio broadcast

HANS MAY (1886–1958)

Der Duft, der eine schöne Frau begleitet

Freiburg February 1956	Südwestfunk Orchestra Stech	Unpublished radio broadcast

Ein Lied geht um die Welt (Wer hat noch nie vom Glück geträumt?)

Munich January 1965	Graunke SO Carste	LP: Karussell 535 009/2430 254/2562 040 LP: Polydor Special 109 616–109 618 LP: DG 2721 230/413 8371 CD: DG 431 1102
Kaiserslautern November 1965	Südwestfunk Orchestra Smola	Unpublished radio broadcast

WALTER MEHRING

Ich lebe für dich

Freiburg September 1956	Südwestfunk Orchestra Stech	Unpublished radio broadcast

WILL MEISEL

Schön ist jeder Tag

Freiburg May 1955	Südwestfunk Orchestra Stech	Unpublished radio broadcast

FRIEDRICH MEYER

O cara Marie (Wenn es Abend wird über den Strassen)

Freiburg February 1956	Südwestfunk Orchestra Stech	Unpublished radio broadcast

ERICH MEYER-HELMUND (1861-1932)

Rokoko-Liebeslied (Gute Nacht, mein holdes süsses Mädchen)

Munich January 1965	Graunke SO Carste	45: Karussell 54 078

CARL MILLOECKER (1842-1899)

Der Bettelstudent, Querschnitt

Berlin October 1959	Role of Jan Köth, L.Schmidt, Töpper, Schock, Neidlinger Arndt Choir Berlin SO Schmidt-Boelcke	LP: Electrola E 83443/STE 83443 LP: EMI 1C 047 28167/1C 037 28167 CD: Laserlight 16 034 Durch diesen Kuss sei unser Bund geweiht LP: EMI EX 29 09883 LP: Angel 6157 CD: EMI CZS 762 9932

Der Bettelstudent, Excerpt (Ich knüpfte manche zarte Bande)

Berlin 1956	Schirrmacher Berlin SO Melichar	LP: Marcato 92 464 LP: Eurodisc OE 88946/IE 70347/96 513/ 300 356.435/301 188.370 CD: Munich Records MR 30007
Munich October 1957	Sailer Munich RO Schmidt-Boelcke	LP: Europäischer Fonoklub 3204

Der Bettelstudent, Excerpt (Darf ich reden?/Ich setz' den Fall)

Berlin 1956	Schirrmacher Berlin SO Melichar	LP: Marcato 92 464 LP: Eurodisc OE 88952
Munich October 1957	Sailer Munich RO Schmidt-Boelcke	LP: Europäischer Fonoklub 3204

Der Bettelstudent, Excerpt (Ich hab' kein Geld, bin vogelfrei)

Munich October 1957	Munich RO Schmidt-Boelcke	LP: Europäischer Fonoklub 3204 LP: Eurodisc IE 70347/OE 88946/XB 86838/ 300 356.435/301 188.370/96 513 CD: Munich Records MR 30007

Der Bettelstudent, Excerpt (Durch diesen Kuss sei unser Bund geweiht)

Stuttgart	Sailer	LP: Vox STGBY 632
1957	Stuttgart PO	
	Mareczek	

Die Dubarry, Excerpts (Mein Weg führt immer mich zu dir zurück; Wie schön ist alles, seit ich dich gefunden)

Munich	Munich RO	Unpublished radio broadcast
June 1962	Moltkau	

HANS MOLTKAU (born 1911)

Geh' nicht fort!

Freiburg	Südwestfunk	Unpublished radio broadcast
February 1955	Orchestra	
	Stech	

Niemals lass' ich dich allein

Freiburg	Südwestfunk	Unpublished radio broadcast
February 1956	Orchestra	
	Stech	

CLAUDIO MONTEVERDI (1567-1643)

L'Orfeo

Hitzacker July 1955 (24 July)	<u>Roles of Apollo/ Pastore II/ Spirito II</u> E.Schmidt,Guilleaume, Krebs, Günter, Roth-Ehrang Hamburg Hochschule Choir Hitzacker Musiktage Instrumentalists Wenzinger	Unpublished radio broadcast
Hannover July 1955 (25-30 July)	Mack-Cosack, Guilleaume, Krebs, Günter, Roth-Ehrang Hamburg Hochschule Choir Hitzacker Musiktage Instrumentalists Wenzinger	LP: DG APM 14 057-14 058/2708 001

WOLFGANG AMADEUS MOZART (1756-1791)

Caro mio Druck und Schluck, Vocal quartet

Freiburg April 1956	Guilleaume, Krebs, Nöcker, Neumeyer, fortepiano	45: DG EPA 37 121 LP: DG APM 14 524

Con ossequio con rispetto, Concert aria

Stuttgart September 1963	SDR Orchestra Müller-Kray	LP: Acanta 23.586 CD: Verona 28044-28045

Cosl fan tutte, Excerpt (Un aura amorosa)

Berlin June 1960	Berlin SO Klobucar <u>Sung in German</u>	LP: EMI 1C 049 30659/EX 29 09883/ 1C 187 29298-29299 LP: Angel 6157 CD: EMI CDC 747 6852

Don Giovanni

Vienna June 1963	<u>Role of Ottavio</u> L.Price, Güden, Sciutti, Wächter, Berry, Kreppel Vienna Opera Chorus VPO Karajan	CD: Verona 27065-27067
Munich December 1963	Kupper, Cunitz, Köth, London, Kohn, Yahia Bavarian State Chorus Munich PO Rieger	Unpublished radio broadcast

230 Wunderlich

Don Giovanni, Querschnitt

Berlin	Hillebrecht,	LP: Odeon O 80583/STO 80583
February 1960	Grümmer, Köth,	LP: EMI 1C 063 28418
	Prey, Kohn,	LP: Turnabout (USA) TV 4030/TV 34030
	Wiemann	CD: EMI CDZ 252 2172/CZS 253 0472
	Deutsche Oper	Excerpts
	Chorus	LP: EMI 1C 187 29298-29299/SHZE 193/
	Berlin SO	HQS 1168/EX 29 09883
	Zanotelli	LP: Angel 6157/60043
	Sung in German	CD: EMI CZS 769 9932

Don Giovanni, Excerpt (Dalla sua pace)

Munich	Munich RO	Unpublished radio broadcast
December 1961	Eichhorn	
	Sung in German	

Don Giovanni, Excerpt (Il mio tesoro)

Berlin	Berlin SO	LP: Electrola E 80769/SME 80769
December 1961	Stein	LP: EMI 1C 063 28420/1C 187 29298-29299/
	Sung in German	HQS 1168/EX 29 09883
		LP: Angel 6157
		CD: EMI CZS 762 9932
Munich	Munich RO	Unpublished radio broadcast
May 1962	Moltkau	
	Sung in German	
Munich	Munich RO	Unpublished radio broadcast
December 1963	Stein	
	Sung in German	
Munich	Munich RO	Unpublished radio broadcast
April 1965	Eichhorn	

Die Entführung aus dem Serail

Hilversum 1957	Role of Belmonte Tyler, Spierenberg, Slys, Hoekman Hilversum Radio Orchestra & Chorus Haitink	Unpublished radio broadcast Tapes probably erased
Salzburg August 1961	Pütz, Holm, Wohlfahrt, Littasy Vienna Opera Chorus Mozarteum Orchestra Kertesz	LP: Period (USA) TE 1102 LP: Melodram MEL 702 CD: Frequenz CMF 2 CD: Movimento musica 051.026 O wie ängstlich CD: Orfeo C394 301B/C408 955R
Buenos Aires September 1961	Rothenberger, Holm, Valori, Böhme Teatro Colon Orchestra & Chorus Wallberg	Unpublished radio broadcast
Salzburg July 1965	Rothenberger, Grist, Unger, Corena Vienna Opera Chorus VPO Mehta	Unpublished radio broadcast

Munich
December 1965
	Köth, Schädle,
	Lenz, Böhme
	Bavarian Radio
	Chorus
	Bavarian State
	Orchestra
	Jochum
		LP: DG LPEM 39 213-39 215/
		    SLPEM 139 213-139 215/2709 021/
		    2726 051
		CD: DG 439 7082
		Excerpts
		LP: DG 135 004/135 127/136 429/2535 277/
		    2535 631/2548 277/2562 040/
		    2563 357/2721 230/413 8371
		CD: DG 423 8682/431 1102/435 1452

Salzburg July 1966	Rothenberger, Grist, Unger, Corena Vienna Opera Chorus VPO Mehta	Unpublished radio broadcast

Die Entführung aus dem Serail, Excerpt (O wie ängstlich)

Berlin July 1960	Berlin SO Klobucar	LP: EMI 1C 187 29298-29299/HQS 1253/ EX 29 09883 LP: Angel 6157 CD: EMI CZS 762 9932 Also used as playback for an SDR TV recording

Die Entführung aus dem Serail, Excerpt (Hier soll ich dich denn sehen?)

Berlin January 1966	Berlin Studio Orchestra Stein	Unpublished radio broadcast

Die Entführung aus dem Serail, Excerpt (Ich baue ganz)

Munich January 1963	Munich RO Stein	Unpublished radio broadcast

La finta giardiniera

Ludwigsburg July 1956	Role of Belfiore Eipperle, O.Moll, Pfeifle, Grefe Württemberg State Orchestra Dünnwald Sung in German	Unpublished radio broadcast

Mass in C minor "Great"

Stuttgart June 1957	Giebel, Bak, Hessenbruch Stuttgart Bach Choir SDR Orchestra Müller-Kray	Unpublished radio broadcast

Misero s sogno!, Concert aria

Stuttgart September 1963	SDR Orchestra Müller-Kray	LP: Acanta 23.586

Regina coeli K276

Salzburg August 1959	Dutoit, Pitzinger, Pacher Salzburg Cathedral Choir Mozarteum Orchestra Messner	Unpublished radio broadcast

Requiem

Ottobeuren June 1958	Giebel, Malaniuk, Rohr Stuttgart Bach Choir SDR Orchestra Müller-Kray	Unpublished radio broadcast
Salzburg August 1960	L.Price, Rössel-Majdan, Berry, Wächter Wiener Singverein VPO Karajan	LP: HRE Records HRE 317 LP: Movimento musica 01.203 CD: Priceless D 16573 CD: Claque GM 2003-2004 CD: Suite CDS 16001
Vienna November 1963	Lipp, Rössel-Majdan, Engen Wiener Singverein VSO Karajan	CD: Melodram MEL 18003 CD: Hunt CDKAR 202 <u>Melodram incorrectly labelled</u> <u>Salzburg 1960</u>

Zaide

Stuttgart October- December 1956	<u>Role of Alonso</u> Stader, Munteanu, Günter SDR Orchestra and Chorus Rischner	LP: Melodram MEL 223 <u>Excerpts</u> CD: Acanta 43.267 CD: Verona 28044-28045

234 Wunderlich

Die Zauberflöte

Hilversum May 1958	Role of Tamino Dongen, Farkas, Naasteren, Derksen Hilversum Radio Orchestra & Chorus Haitink	Unpublished radio broadcast
Salzburg August 1960	Fölser, Köth, Berry, Frick, Wächter Vienna Opera Chorus VPO Keilberth	Unpublished radio broadcast

Berlin
June 1964
	Lear, Peters,
	Fischer-Dieskau,
	Crass, Hotter
	RIAS Choir
	BPO
	Böhm
		LP: DG LPM 18 981-18 983/
		    SLPM 138 981-138 983/2709 017/
		    2720 058/2740 108/2740 207/2740 222
		CD: DG 419 5662/429 8772/435 3952
		Excerpts
		LP: DG 135 004/136 440/2537 003/
		    2562 040/2721 081/2721 230/413 8371
		CD: DG 431 1102

Munich July 1964	Rothenberger, Köth, Prey, Kohn, Engen Bavarian State Chorus Munich PO Rieger	Unpublished radio broadcast

Die Zauberflöte, Querschnitt

Hamburg
1958
	Giebel, Vivarelli,
	Roth-Ehrang,
	Günter
	Philharmonisches
	Staatsorchester
	and Chorus
	Rother
		LP: Europäischer Fonoklub 1134/1902
		LP: Eurodisc 201 023.250
		Excerpts
		LP: Eurodisc OU 27037/KR 70259/XA 25289/
		    XA 77381/XA 85844/XB 25959/XB 86838/
		    XN 87790/300 356.435/300 648.370/
		    301 185.370/96 513
		CD: Eurodisc GD 69018

Die Zauberflöte, Excerpt (Dies Bildnis ist bezaubernd schön)

Stuttgart April 1959	SDR Orchestra Schuricht	LP: Acanta 23.267 CD: Acanta 43.267 <u>Also used as playback for a TV recording</u>
Berlin June 1960	Berlin SO Klobucar	LP: EMI 1C 187 29298-29299/SHZE 193/ HQS 1168/EX 29 09883 LP: Angel 6157/60043 CD: EMI CDC 747 6852
Munich December 1961	Munich RO Eichhorn	Unpublished radio broadcast

FRITZ NEUMEYER (1900-1983)

8 Studentenlieder für eine Tenorstimme und Streicher

Saarbrücken July 1960	Saar Chamber Orchestra Ristenpart	LP: EMI 1C 063 30145

ADOLF NEUENDORFF (1843-1897)

Der Rattenfänger (Wandern, ach wandern, durch Berg und Tal)

Berlin January 1962	Berlin SO Eisbrenner	LP: EMI SHZE 193 LP: Angel 60043 CD: EMI CZS 762 9932

OTTO NICOLAI (1810-1849)

Die lustigen Weiber von Windsor

Munich
February
1962
	Role of Fenton
	Litz, Pütz, Lenz,
	Frick, Engen,
	Gutstein
	Bavarian State
	Orchestra & Chorus
	Heger
		LP: Electrola E 91265-91267/
		    STE 91267-91268
		LP: HMV ALP 2031-2032/ASD 580-581
		LP: EMI 1C 183 30191-30193/
		    1C 197 30191-30193
		CD: EMI CMS 769 3482
		Excerpts
		LP: Electrola E 80769/STE 80769
		LP: EMI 1C 063 28420/1C 063 29003/
		    1C 187 29298-29299/SHZE 193/HQS 1168/
		    EX 29 09883
		LP: Angel 6157/60043/36149
		CD: EMI CZS 762 9932

Die lustigen Weiber von Windsor, Excerpt (Horch, die Lerche singt im Hain!)

Stuttgart December 1959	SDR Orchestra Rischner	Unpublished radio broadcast <u>Also used as playback for a TV recording</u>
Munich May 1962	Munich RO Moltkau	Unpublished radio broadcast

CARL ORFF (1895-1982)

Antigonae

Stuttgart March 1956	<u>Role of Theban Elder</u> Plümacher, Mödl, Stolze, Traxel, Uhde, Rohr, Württemberg State Orchestra & Chorus Leitner	Unpublished radio broadcast

Oedipus der Tyrann

Stuttgart December 1959	<u>Role of Tiresias</u> Varnay, Stolze, Domgraf-Fassbaender, Bauer Württemberg State Orchestra & Chorus Leitner	Unpublished radio broadcast

GIOVANNI PAISIELLO (1740-1816)

La molinara, Excerpt (Nel cor più non mi sento)

Kaiserslautern January 1959	Verlooy Südwestfunk-Unterhaltungs-Orchester Smola	Unpublished radio broadcast

GIOVANNI BATTISTA PERGOLESI (1710-1736)

Il maestro di musica

Vienna February 1963	<u>Role of Lamberto</u> Sciutti, Berry VSO Swarowsky <u>Sung in German</u>	Unpublished video recording

HANS PFITZNER (1869-1949)

Von deutscher Seele

Stuttgart October 1958	Kupper, Bence Denger SDR Orchestra Stuttgart Philharmonic Choir Mende	Unpublished radio broadcast <u>Excerpt</u> CD: Verona 28044-28045
Munich December 1965	Giebel, Töpper, Wiener Bavarian Radio Orchestra & Chorus Keilberth	LP: DG 2707 027 CD: DG 437 0332

Palestrina

Vienna December 1964	<u>Role of Palestrina</u> Janowitz, C.Ludwig, Stolze, Kreppel, Wiener, Welter Vienna Opera Chorus VPO Heger	CD: Myto MCD 92259

MANUEL PONCE (1882-1948)

Estrellita (Sternenschein macht heut' nacht die Nacht zum Wunder)

Kaiserslautern November 1965	Südwestfunk Orchestra Smola	Unpublished radio broadcast

GIACOMO PUCCINI (1858-1924)

La Bohème, Querschnitt

Berlin
September 1956
	Role of Rodolfo
	Eipperle, Pütz,
	Koffmane, Brauer,
	Roth-Ehrang
	Deutsche Oper
	Orchestra & Chorus
	Kraus
	Sung in German
		LP: Europäischer Fonoklub 1105
		LP: Eurodisc KR 70259/ZR 75871/
		    201 021.250
		Che gelida manina
		LP: Eurodisc OU 27037/XA 25289/XQ 28526/
		    300 356.435/301 185.370/96 513

Berlin
June 1961
	Rothenberger,
	Pütz, G.Völker,
	Cordes, Frick
	Berlin SO
	Komische Oper
	Chorus
	Klobucar
	Sung in German
		LP: Columbia (Germany) C 80637/STC 80637
		LP: EMI 1C 063 28529
		CD: EMI CDZ 252 2132/CZS 253 0472
		Excerpts
		LP: Electrola E 80847/SME 80847
		LP: EMI 1C 063 28173/SHZE 110/SHZE 193/
		    1C 187 29298-29299/EX 29 09883
		    1C 057 46116/1C 137 46111-46117
		LP: Angel 6157/60043
		CD: EMI CDC 747 6852/CZS 762 9932
		    CZS 252 3492

La Bohème, Excerpt (Che gelida manina)

Munich December 1963	Munich RO Stein Sung in German	Unpublished radio broadcast

La Bohème, Excerpt (Che penna infame!)

Munich December 1961	Prey Munich RO Eichhorn Sung in German	LP: DG 2535 801/2700 709/2721 230/413 8371 CD: DG 431 1102/435 1452
Munich September 1962	Prey Munich RO Eichhorn Sung in German	Unpublished radio broadcast

Madama Butterfly, Querschnitt

Berlin 1956	Role of Pinkerton Eipperle, Hilbert, Zilliken Deutsche Oper Orchestra & Chorus Kraus Sung in German	LP: Europäischer Fonoklub 1102 LP: Eurodisc 201 022.250/ZR 75873 Addio fiorito asil LP: Eurodisc KR 70259/XA 25289/96 513/ 300 356.435/301 185.370
Berlin April 1961	Lorengar, Wagner, Prey Berlin SO Komische Oper Chorus Klobucar Sung in German	LP: Columbia (Germany) C 80632/STC 80632 LP: EMI 1C 063 29000 CD: EMI CDM 769 2142 Excerpts LP: Electrola E 80847/SME 80847 LP: EMI 1C 063 28173/1C 187 29298-29299/ SHZE 193/EX 29 09883 LP: Angel 6157/60043 CD: EMI CZS 762 9932

Madama Butterfly, Excerpt (Bimba degli occhi)

Munich April 1965	Lorengar Munich RO Eichhorn Sung in German	Unpublished radio broadcast

Tosca, Excerpt (Recondita armonia)

Berlin 1958	Berlin SO Kraus Sung in German	LP: Europäischer Fonoklub 4232 LP: Eurodisc 300 356.435/96 513/ 301 185.370

Tosca, Excerpt (E lucevan le stelle)

Berlin 1958	Berlin SO Kraus Sung in German	LP: Europäischer Fonoklub 4232 LP: Eurodisc XB 25965/300 356.435/ 301 185.370/96 513
Kaiserslautern November 1965	Südwestfunk Orchestra Smola Sung in German	LP: DG 2535 801/2700 709/2721 230/413 8371 CD: DG 431 1102/435 1452

Turandot, Excerpt (Non piangere, Liù!)

Berlin	Berlin SO	LP: Europäischer Fonoklub 4232
1958	Kraus	LP: Eurodisc KR 70259/XB 25965/96 513/
	Sung in German	300 356.435/301 185.370

Turandot, Excerpt (Nessun dorma)

Berlin	Berlin SO	LP: Europäischer Fonoklub 4232
1958	Kraus	LP: Eurodisc KR 70259/XA 25289/XB 86838/
	Sung in German	300 356.435/96 513/301 185.370

GUNTER RAPHAEL (1903-1960)

Palmström-Sonate

Stuttgart	Reinhardt	Unpublished radio broadcast
October 1957	Instrumentalists	

FRED RAYMOND (1900-1954)

Maske in Blau, Excerpts (Schau einer schönen Frau; Maske in Blau)

Berlin	FFB-Orchester	LP: Europäischer Fonoklub 3175
October 1956	Becker	LP: Eurodisc IE 70347/OE 88946/96 513/
		300 356.435/301 185.370
		CD: Munich Records MR 30007

JOHANN FRIEDRICH REICHHARDT (1752-1814)

Brenno, Excerpts (Santi numi del cielo/Stelle! Che dici?/Cara! Che dir mi vuoi?)

Kaiserslautern	Verlooy	Unpublished radio broadcast
January 1959	Südwestfunk	
	Orchestra	
	Smola	

ADAM RENER (1485-1520)

Mein höchste Frucht

Mainz   Instrumentalists   Unpublished radio broadcast
Date uncertain

HERMANN REUTTER (1900-1985)

Tryptichon for tenor, choir and orchestra

Stuttgart   SDR Orchestra   Unpublished radio broadcast
June 1960   and Chorus
                   Müller-Kray

VINCENZO RIGHINI (1756-1812)

Alcide al bivio, Excerpt (Questo agevole è amero/Dei clementi, amici Dei!)

Kaiserslautern   Südwestfunk-   Unpublished radio broadcast
March 1957   Unterhaltungs-
                   Orchester
                   Smola

Alcide al bivio, Excerpt (Alme belle, fuggite prudenti!)

Kaiserslautern   Verlooy, Bence,   Unpublished radio broadcast
January 1959   Nöcker
                   Südwestfunk-
                   Unterhaltungs-
                   Orchester
                   Smola

MARC ROLAND

Unter dem Sternenzelt, from the film Ferien vom Ich

Berlin	Berlin SO	CD: Eurodisc GD 69018
1957	Becker	CD: Munich Records MR 30007

JOHANN ROSENMUELLER (1619-1684)

Die Klagelieder Jeremias (Lamentationes Jeremiae)

Stuttgart   Instrumentalists   CD: Bella voce BLV 107.003
March 1957

GIOACCHINO ROSSINI (1792-1868)

Il barbiere di Siviglia

Munich December 1959	Role of Almaviva Köth, Gerhein, Prey, Proebstl, Hotter Bavarian State Orchestra & Chorus Keilberth Sung in German	Unpublished video recording
Vienna April 1966	Grist, H.Konetzni, Kunz, Wächter, Czerwenka Vienna Opera Chorus VPO Böhm Sung in German	LP: Teatro dischi TD 502-503 CD: Myto MCD 91752 Teatro dischi incorrectly dated 1964

Il barbiere di Siviglia, Excerpt (All' idea di quel metallo)

Munich September 1962	Prey Munich RO Eichhorn <u>Sung in German</u>	LP: DG 2535 801/ 413 8371 CD: DG 431 1102/435 1452
Munich December 1963	Grumbach Munich RO Stein <u>Sung in German</u>	Unpublished radio broadcast

Il barbiere di Siviglia, Excerpt (Ah, quel colpo inaspettato!)

Munich December 1961	Köth, Prey Munich RO Eichhorn <u>Sung in German</u>	Unpublished radio broadcast
Munich September 1962	Köth, Prey Munich RO Eichhorn <u>Sung in German</u>	LP: DG 2700 709/2535 801/2721 230

La Cenerentola, Excerpt (Mi seduce, m'innamora quella sua semplicità)

Munich September 1962	Köth Munich RO Eichhorn <u>Sung in German</u>	Unpublished radio broadcast

La danza (Già la luna è in mezzo al mare)

Munich January 1965	Graunke SO Carste	LP: Karussell 535 009/2430 254 LP: Polydor Special 109 616-109 618

ALESSANDRO SCARLATTI (1660-1725)

La rosaura, Excerpt (Quel povero core!)

Kaiserslautern January 1959	Südwestfunk Orchestra Smola	Unpublished radio broadcast

FRANZ SCHMIDT (1874-1939)

Das Buch mit sieben Siegeln

Salzburg August 1959	Güden, Malaniuk, Dermota, Berry Wiener Singverein VPO Mitropoulos	LP: Melodram MEL 705 CD: Melodram MEL 27078 CD: Sony SM2K 68442 Excerpt CD: Verona 28044-28045

LUDWIG SCHMIEDSEDER (1904-1971)

I hab' die schönen Mäderln net erfunden

Vienna June 1966	Volksoper Orchestra Stolz	LP: Heliodor (USA) H 25051/HS 25051 LP: Polydor Special 109 616-109 618 LP: DG 413 8371 CD: DG 435 1452

FRANZ SCHUBERT (1797-1828)

Mass No 6 in E flat

Berlin April 1960	Lorengar, Allen, M.Schmidt, Greindl St Hedwig's Choir BPO Leinsdorf	LP: Electrola K 80725/STK 80725 LP: EMI 1C 053 80005

Fierrabras

Bern April 1959	Role of Eginhard Geissler, Kahmann, Plümacher, Timper, Mielsch, Rohr, Wolansky Bern Orchestra and Chorus Müller-Kray	CD: Myto MCD 89001 Excerpts CD: Verona 28044-28045

SALZBURGER FESTSPIELE 1959

DIE SCHWEIGSAME FRAU

KOMISCHE OPER IN DREI AUFZÜGEN
FREI NACH BEN JONSON VON STEFAN ZWEIG

MUSIK VON
RICHARD STRAUSS

DIRIGENT
KARL BÖHM

INSZENIERUNG
GÜNTHER RENNERT

BÜHNENBILD
TEO OTTO

KOSTÜME
ERNI KNIEPERT

ORCHESTER
DIE WIENER PHILHARMONIKER
CHOR DER WIENER STAATSOPER

DIE SCHWEIGSAME FRAU

Komische Oper in drei Aufzügen
Frei nach Ben Jonson von Stefan Zweig

MUSIK VON RICHARD STRAUSS
Opus 80

Sir Morosus	. . . .	Hans Hotter
Seine Haushälterin	. . . . . .	Georgine v. Milinkovic
Der Barbier	. . . .	Hermann Prey
Henry Morosus	. . . .	Fritz Wunderlich
Aminta, seine Frau	. . . .	Hilde Güden
Isotta	. . . .	Pierette Alarie
Carlotta	Komödianten	Hetty Plümacher
Morbio	. . . .	Josef Knapp
Vanuzzi	. . . .	Carl Dönch
Farfallo	. . . .	Alois Pernerstorfer

Chor der Komödianten und Nachbarn

Ort der Handlung:
Zimmer des Sir Morosus in einem Vorort Londons

Zeit: Nach 1780

Größere Pause nach dem ersten Aufzug

Kleinere Pause nach dem zweiten Aufzug

Der offizielle Almanach „Salzburg — Festspiele 1959" ist auch für Sie der unentbehrliche Ratgeber
The official almanac "Salzburg Festivals 1959" is an indispensable guide for all Festival visitors
L'almanach officiel «Salzbourg Festival 1959» est indispensable à tous ceux qui s'intéressent au Festival

Die Wunderinsel (Alfonso und Estrella), Querschnitt

Stuttgart November 1958– February 1959	Role of Ferdinand Sailer, Freymann, Brauer, McDaniel, Linke SDR Orchestra and Chorus Dünnwald	Unpublished radio broadcast

An die Laute (Leiser, leiser, kleine Laute!)

Schwetzingen May 1965	Giesen	Unpublished radio broadcast
Salzburg August 1965	Giesen	LP: Acanta 40.23529 CD: Acanta 43.529 CD: Myto MCD 89011
Munich October– November 1965	Giesen	LP: DG LPEM 39 125/SLPEM 139 125/413 8371 CD: DG 435 1452
Hannover March 1966	Giesen	CD: Myto MCD 93278
Edinburgh September 1966	Giesen	Unpublished radio broadcast

An die Musik (Du holde Kunst, in wieviel grauen Stunden)

Munich November 1965	Giesen	LP: DG 2535 614/2535 656/2707 031/ 2721 230 CD: DG 435 1452/447 4522
Hannover March 1966	Giesen	CD: Myto MCD 93278
Edinburgh September 1966	Giesen	CD: Myto MCD 89011 CD: Verona 28044-28045

Schubert Lieder/continued

An Silvia (Was ist Silvia, saget an?)

Schwetzingen May 1965	Giesen	Unpublished radio broadcast
Salzburg August 1965	Giesen	LP: Acanta 40.23529 CD: Acanta 43.529 CD: Myto MCD 89011
Munich October- November 1965	Giesen	LP: DG 2535 614/2535 656/2707 031 CD: DG 429 9332/435 1452
Hannover March 1966	Giesen	CD: Myto MCD 93278
Edinburgh September 1966	Giesen	Unpublished radio broadcast

Der Einsame (Wenn meine Grillen schwirren)

Schwetzingen May 1965	Giesen	Unpublished radio broadcast
Salzburg August 1965	Giesen	LP: Acanta 40.23529 CD: Acanta 43.529 CD: Myto MCD 89011
Munich October- November 1965	Giesen	LP: DG 2535 614/2707 031 CD: DG 429 9332/435 1452/447 4522
Hannover March 1966	Giesen	CD: Myto MCD 93278
Edinburgh September 1966	Giesen	Unpublished radio broadcast

Die Forelle (In einem Bächlein helle)

Munich October- November 1965	Giesen	LP: DG LPEM 39 125/SLPEM 139 125/ 135 005/2721 230/413 8371 CD: DG 423 9562/435 1452
Edinburgh September 1966	Giesen	Unpublished radio broadcast

Schubert Lieder/continued

Frühlingsglaube (Die linden Lüfte sind erwacht)

Munich October- November 1965	Giesen	LP: DG 2535 614/2535 656/2707 031/ 2721 230 CD: DG 423 9562/435 1452/447 4522
Hannover March 1966	Giesen	CD: Myto MCD 93278

Heidenröslein (Sah ein Knab' ein Röslein steh'n)

Munich October- November 1965	Giesen	LP: DG 2535 614/2707 031/2721 230 CD: DG 423 9562/431 1102/435 1452

Ihr Bild/Schwanengesang (Ich stand in dunkeln Träumen)

Mainz November 1962	Reinhardt	LP: EMI 1C 063 30145

Im Abendrot (O wie schön ist diese Welt!)

Salzburg August 1965	Giesen	LP: Acanta 40.23529 CD: Acanta 43.529 CD: Myto MCD 89011
Munich October- November 1965	Giesen	LP: DG LPEM 39 125/SLPEM 139 125/135 005/ 135 007/2535 614/2721 230 CD: DG 429 9332/435 1452

Liebhaber in allen Gestalten (Ich wollt', ich wär' ein Fisch!)

Munich October- November 1965	Giesen	LP: DG 2707 031 CD: DG 429 9332/435 1452/447 4522

Schubert Lieder/continued

Lied eines Schiffers an die Dioskuren (Dioskuren, Zwillingssterne!)

Schwetzingen May 1965	Giesen	Unpublished radio broadcast
Salzburg August 1965	Giesen	LP: Acanta 40.23529 CD: Acanta 43.529 CD: Myto MCD 89011
Munich October- November 1965	Giesen	LP: DG LPEM 39 125/SLPEM 139 125/ 135 014/2535 614/ 413 8371 CD: DG 429 9332/435 1452
Hannover March 1966	Giesen	CD: Myto MCD 93278
Edinburgh September 1966	Giesen	Unpublished radio broadcast

Der Musensohn (Durch Feld und Wald zu schweifen)

Stuttgart 1956	Reinhardt	LP: Eurodisc XD 86083/XN 87786/96 513/ 300 356.435/301 185.370 CD: Eurodisc GD 69312
Schwetzingen May 1965	Giesen	Unpublished radio broadcast
Salzburg August 1965	Giesen	LP: Acanta 40.23529 CD: Acanta 43.529 CD: Myto MCD 89011
Munich October- November 1965	Giesen	LP: DG LPEM 39 125/SLPEM 139 125/135 007/ 2535 614/2535 656/ 413 8371 CD: DG 429 9332/435 1452
Hannover March 1966	Giesen	CD: Myto MCD 93278

Schubert Lieder/continued

Nachtstück (Wenn über Berge sich der Nebel breitet)

Schwetzingen May 1965	Giesen	Unpublished radio broadcast
Salzburg August 1965	Giesen	LP: Acanta 40.23529 CD: Acanta 43.529 CD: Myto MCD 89011
Hannover March 1966	Giesen	CD: Myto MCD 93278
Edinburgh September 1966	Giesen	Unpublished radio broadcast

Die schöne Müllerin, song cycle

Berlin August 1957	K.Stolze	LP: Europäischer Fonoklub 3171-3172 LP: Eurodisc XA 88643/XD 86083 CD: Eurodisc GD 69312 Excerpts LP: Eurodisc XF 25490/200 941.315/96 513/ 300 356.435/301 185.370
Cologne March 1959	K.Stolze	Unpublished radio broadcast
Stuttgart March 1964	Giesen	Unpublished radio broadcast
Cologne October 1965	Giesen	CD: Verona 2701
Munich July 1966	Giesen	LP: DG 2707 031/2535 133/2538 347/413 8371 CD: DG 423 9562/435 1452/447 4522 Excerpts LP: DG 135 014/2721 230

Ständchen (Horch, horch, die Lerch'!)

Stuttgart 1956	Reinhardt	CD: Eurodisc OU 27037/XF 25490/96 513/ 200 607.250/300 356.435/301 185.370 CD: Eurodisc GD 69312
Mainz November 1962	Reinhardt	LP: EMI 1C 063 30145

Schubert Lieder/concluded

Ständchen/Schwanengesang (Leise flehen meine Lieder)

Munich	Giesen	LP: DG 2535 614/2707 031/2721 230
October–		CD: DG 429 9332/435 1452/447 4522
November 1965		

Ungeduld/Die schöne Müllerin (Ich schnitt es gern in alle Rinden ein)

| Stuttgart | Reinhardt | LP: Eurodisc OK 25290 |
| 1956 | | |

| Salzburg | Giesen | LP: Acanta 40.23529 |
| August 1965 | | CD: Acanta 43.529 |

| Edinburgh | Giesen | CD: Myto MCD 89011 |
| September 1966 | | CD: Verona 28044-28045 |

Other versions of Ungeduld included in complete cycle of Die schöne Müllerin listed previously

Der Wachtelschlag (Horch, wie schallt's dorten so lieblich hervor!)

| Munich | L.Kusche | Unpublished video recording |
| Date uncertain | | |

Wiegenlied (Schlafe, schlafe, holder süsser Knabe!)

| Munich | Graunke SO | 45: Karussell 54 078 |
| January 1965 | Carste | |

ROBERT SCHUMANN (1810-1856)

Dichterliebe, song cycle

Vienna May 1963	H. Schmidt	Unpublished radio broadcast
Schwetzingen May 1965	Giesen	Unpublished radio broadcast
Salzburg August 1965	Giesen	LP: Acanta 40.23529 CD: Acanta 43.529
Munich October- November 1965	Giesen	LP: DG LPEM 39 125/SLPEM 139 125/ 413 8371 CD: DG 429 9332/435 1452 Excerpts LP: DG 2535 614
Hannover March 1966	Giesen	CD: Myto MCD 93278
Edinburgh September 1966	Giesen	CD: Myto MCD 89011

Die Lotosblume ängstigt

Edinburgh September 1966	Giesen	CD: Myto MCD 89011 CD: Verona 28044-28045

Duets: Er und sie; Ich denke dein

Stuttgart 1956	Sailer Reinhardt	LP: Eurodisc OK 25290

Duets: Tanzlied; Unterm Fenster

Stuttgart 1956	Sailer Reinhardt	LP: Europäischer Fonoklub 4304 LP: Eurodisc OK 25290

HEINRICH SCHUETZ (1585-1672)

Lobe den Herren, meine Seele!

Freiburg June 1953	Mikulicz, Ramm, Hackbarth Instrumentalists Millies	Unpublished radio broadcast

Sinfoniae sacrae: Es steh' Gott auf, dass seine Feind' zerstreut werden;
Was betrübst du dich, meine Seele?

Stuttgart May 1956	Michaelis Instrumentalists	Unpublished radio broadcast

Weihnachtsmotetten: Pro hoc magno misterio; Supereminet omnem scientiam

Stuttgart December 1956	Guilleaume, H.Münch, Weidermann Instrumentalists	Unpublished radio broadcast

LUDWIG SENFL (1490-1543)

Ein alt bös Weib; Entlaubet ist der Walde; Ich armes Käuzlein kleine;
Lust hab ich gehabt zur Musica; Unsäglich Schmerz; Wie wohl ich trag

Freiburg October 1954	Instrumentalists	Unpublished radio broadcast

RUDOLF SIECZYNSKI (1879-1952)

Wien, Wien, nur du allein

Vienna June 1966	Volksoper Orchestra Stolz	LP: Heliodor (USA) H 25051/HS 25051 LP: Polydor Special 109 616-109 618 LP: DG 413 8371 CD: DG 435 1452

BEDRICH SMETANA (1824-1884)

The Bartered Bride

Bamberg
May 1962
and Berlin
October 1962
	Role of Jenik
	Lorengar, Wagner,
	Frick, Cordes,
	Sardi
	RIAS Choir
	Bamberg SO
	Kempe
	Sung in German
		LP: Electrola E 91226-91228/
		    STE 91226-91228
		LP: HMV ALP 1971-1973/ASD 522-524
		LP: Angel 3642
		LP: EMI 1C153 28922-28923/HQS1132-1134 /
		    EX 29 12953
		CD: EMI CDS 749 2792/CMS 764 0022
		Excerpts
		LP: Electrola E 80746/STE 80746/SME 80769/
		    E 80847/SME 80847
		LP: EMI 1C 063 28173/1C 063 28420/
		    1C 063 29002/1C 063 30144/EX 29 09883/
		    1C 148 31205/1C187 29298-29299
		LP: Angel 6157
		CD: EMI CZS 767 1872/CZS 762 9932
		    CZS 767 1872

The Bartered Bride, Excerpt (It must succeed! Everything shall go according to our hearts' desire)

Munich May 1962	Munich RO Moltkau Sung in German	Unpublished radio broadcast

The Bartered Bride, Excerpt (My dearest love, attention now!)

Munich April 1965	Lorengar Munich RO Eichhorn Sung in German	Unpublished radio broadcast

The Bartered Bride, Excerpt (Now in happiness and grief)

Berlin January 1966	Hallstein Deutsche Oper Chorus Berlin Studio Orchestra Stein Sung in German	Unpublished radio broadcast Also used as playback for a TV recording

The Bartered Bride, Excerpt (Just listen to me for a moment, my son!)

Stuttgart October 1956	Linke Württemberg State Orchestra Dünnwald Sung in German	Unpublished radio broadcast
Berlin March 1962	Böhme Berlin SO Stein Sung in German	Unpublished radio broadcast Also used as playback to a TV recording
Berlin January 1966	Böhme Berlin Studio Orchestra Stein Sung in German	Unpublished radio broadcast Also used as playback for a TV recording
Munich February 1966	Böhme Munich RO Köhler Sung in German	Unpublished radio broadcast

MISCHA SPOLIANSKI (1898-1985)

Heute nacht oder nie

Munich January 1965	Graunke SO Carste	LP: Karussell 535 009 LP: Polydor Special 109 616-109 618 LP: DG 2721 230/413 8371 CD: DG 435 1452
Munich February 1966	Munich RO Köhler	Unpublished radio broadcast

ALEXANDER STEINBRECHER (1910-1982)

Ich kenn' ein kleines Wegerl im Helenental

Vienna June 1966	Volksoper Orchestra Stolz	LP: Heliodor (USA) H 25051/HS 25051 LP: Polydor Special 109 616-109 618 LP: DG 413 8371 CD: DG 435 1452

ROBERT STOLZ (1880-1975)

Frühjahrsparade, Excerpt (Wien wird erst schön bei Nacht)

Vienna June 1966	Volksoper Orchestra Stolz	LP: Karussell 535 009/2415 030 LP: Heliodor (USA) H 25051/HS 25051 LP: Polydor Special 109 616-109 618 LP: DG 413 8371

Im Prater blüh'n wieder die Bäume

Vienna June 1966	Vienna Opera Chorus Volksoper Orchestra Stolz	LP: Heliodor (USA) H 25051/HS 25051 LP: Polydor Special 109 616-109 618 LP: DG 413 8371 CD: DG 435 1452

In Wien gibt's manch' winziges Gasserl

Munich August 1966	Spilar-Schrammeln	LP: Karussell 2415 030 LP: Heliodor (USA) H 25051/HS 25051 LP: Polydor Special 109 616-109 618

Mädi, Excerpts (Mädi, mein kleines Mädi!; Zum ersten Mal allein)

Kaiserslautern January 1954	Hübner Südwestfunk Orchestra Smola	Unpublished radio broadcast

Ob blond oder braun, ich lieb' alle Frau'n

Munich January 1965	Graunke SO Carste	LP: Karussell 535 009 LP: Polydor Special 109 616-109 618 LP: DG 2721 230/413 8371 CD: DG 435 1452
Munich February 1966	Munich RO Köhler	CD: Originals SH 866

Prinzessin Ti-Ti-Pa, Excerpt (Einmal hat mir zur Frühlingszeit das Glück gelacht)

Kaiserslautern January 1954	Südwestfunk Orchestra Smola	Unpublished radio broadcast

Signorina, Excerpts (Arrivederci, bella Italia!; Zwei sind verliebt und wissen's nicht)

Kaiserslautern July 1955	Assmann Südwestfunk Orchestra Smola	Unpublished radio broadcast

Die Tanzgräfin, Excerpt (Mein Herz ruft immer nur nach dir, o Marita!)

Munich January 1965	Graunke SO Carste	LP: Karussell 2415 030 LP: Polydor Special 109 616-109 618

Venus in Seide, Excerpt (Erst hab' ich ihr Komplimente gemacht)

Kaiserslautern January 1954	Südwestfunk Orchestra Smola	CD: Verona 28044-28045

Zauber der Bohème, Excerpt (Weine nicht, bricht eine schöne Frau dir das Herz)

Munich May-June 1965	Graunke SO Carste	LP: Karussell 2435 108 LP: Heliodor (USA) H 25063/HS 25063 LP: Polydor Special 109 616-109 618

OSCAR STRAUS (1870-1954)

Ein Walzertraum

Cologne April 1959	Role of Niki Cramer, Fahberg, Stanorski WDR Orchestra Marszalek	LP: RCA VL 30318 CD: Sonia 74505 Also used as playback for a TV recording

JOHANN STRAUSS (1825-1899)

Eine Nacht in Venedig, Querschnitt

Berlin	Role of Caramello	LP: Odeon O 83445/STO 83445
June-	Otto, Schirrmacher,	LP: EMI 1C 047 28127
September 1960	Schock, Mercker,	Excerpts
	G.Völker	LP: EMI 1C 061 28064/HQS 1168/EX 29 09883
	Arndt Choir	LP: Angel 6157
	Berlin SO	CD: EMI CZS 762 9932
	F.Walter	

Eine Nacht in Venedig, Excerpt (Treu sein, das liegt mir nicht)

Berlin	Berlin SO	LP: Europäischer Fonoklub 3170
1956	Melichar	LP: Eurodisc OE 88946/XF 76499/96 513/
		300 356.435/301 188.370
		CD: Eurodisc GD 69018
		CD: Munich Records MR 30007
Munich	Munich RO	Unpublished radio broadcast
June 1962	Moltkau	

Eine Nacht in Venedig, Excerpt (Komm in die Gondel)

Berlin	Chorus	LP: Europäischer Fonoklub 3170
1956	Berlin SO	LP: Eurodisc IE 70347/OE 88946/OU 27037/
	Melichar	XB 86838/XF 80397/XN 87794/XQ 27252/
		300 356.435/96 513/301.185.370
		CD: Eurodisc GD 69018
		CD: Munich Records MR 30007

Eine Nacht in Venedig, Excerpt (Ach, wie so herrlich zu schau'n!)

Munich	Chorus	LP: Europäischer Fonoklub 3170
October 1957	Munich RO	LP: Eurodisc OE 88952/OU 27037/
	Schmidt-Boelcke	XA 85844/XF 80397/300.356.435/
		96 513/301 185.370
		CD: Eurodisc GD 69018
		CD: Munich Records MR 30007

Eine Nacht in Venedig, Excerpt (Willkommen, alte Freunde!)

Berlin	Berlin SO	LP: Eurodisc XF 80397
1956	Melichar	

Eine Nacht in Venedig, Excerpt (Sei mir gegrüsst, du holdes Venezia!)

Munich June 1962	Munich RO Moltkau	Unpublished radio broadcast

Die Fledermaus

Cologne September 1959	Role of Eisenstein Fahberg, Bartos, Francl, Fehringer, Lins, Kusche WDR Orchestra and Chorus Marszalek	LP: RCA VL 30318 LP: Acanta 23.567 CD: Sonia 74505 Also used as playback for a TV recording

Die Fledermaus, Querschnitt

Stuttgart 1956	Roles of Alfred and Eisenstein Robert, Paul, Samland SDR Orchestra and Chorus Müller-Kray	LP: Europäischer Fonoklub 3110 LP: Acanta 40.229032

Die Fledermaus, Excerpt (Trinke, Liebchen, trinke schnell!)

Munich February 1966	Pütz, Böhme Munich RO Köhler	CD: Originals SH 866

Der lustige Krieg, Excerpt (Nur für Natur hegte sie Sympathie)

Stuttgart 1957	Stuttgart PO Mareczek	LP: Vox STGBY 632 CD: ZYX music CLS 42012

Der Zigeunerbaron

Munich June 1962	Role of Barinkay Talmar, Brühl, Ehre, P.Schmidt, Millowitsch Gärtnerplatz Choir Belgrade SO R.Wilhelm	Unpublished video recording Playback for a cinema film

Der Zigeunerbaron, Excerpt (Als flotter Geist)

Munich October 1957	Munich RO Schmidt-Boelcke	LP: Europäischer Fonoklub 3204 LP: Eurodisc IE 70347/OE 88946/OE 88952/ OU 27037/XB 86838/300 356.435/ 96 513/301 188.370 CD: Eurodisc GD 69018 CD: Munich Records MR 30007

Der Zigeunerbaron, Excerpt (Wer uns getraut)

Munich October 1957	Sailer Munich RO Schmidt-Boelcke	LP: Europäischer Fonoklub 3204 LP: Eurodisc OE 88952/201 981.315/96 513/ 300 356.435/301 188.370

Draussen in Sievering

Vienna June 1966	Vienna Opera Chorus Volksoper Orchestra Stolz	LP: Karussell 535 009 LP: Heliodor (USA) H 25051/HS 25051 LP: Polydor Special 109 616-109 618 LP: DG 413 8371 CD: DG 435 1452

RICHARD STRAUSS (1864-1949)

Barcarole (Um der fallenden Ruder Spitzen)

Munich   L.Kusche   Unpublished video recording
Date uncertain

Capriccio

Vienna   Role of Sänger   Unpublished radio broadcast
March 1964   Della Casa,
                  C.Ludwig, Popp,
                  Kmennt, Kerns,
                  Berry, Wiener
                  VPO
                  Prêtre

Daphne

Vienna   Role of Leukippos   LP: DG LPM 18 956-18 957/
May 1964   Güden, Streich,   SLPM 138 956-138 957/2707 019/
                  Little, King,   2721 190/2726 090
                  Schöffler   CD: DG 423 5792/445 3322/445 4912
                  Vienna Opera Chorus
                  VSO
                  Böhm

Munich   Woytowicz, Töpper,   Unpublished radio broadcast
September 1964   King, Frick   Also playback for a TV recording
                  Bavarian Radio
                  Orchestra & Chorus
                  Keilberth

Vienna   Güden, Streich,   Unpublished radio broadcast
April 1965   Little, King,
                  Schöffler
                  Vienna Opera Chorus
                  VSO
                  Böhm

264 Wunderlich

Die Frau ohne Schatten

Vienna June 1964	Role of Youth Rysanek, C.Ludwig, G.Hoffman, J.Thomas, Berry, Kreppel Vienna Opera Chorus VPO Karajan	CD: Nuova Era 2288-2290 CD: Hunt CDKAR 207

Freundliche Vision (Nicht im Schlafe hab' ich das geträumt)

Munich Date uncertain	L.Kusche	Unpublished video recording

Heimliche Aufforderung (Auf, hebe die funkelnde Schale empor zum Mund!)

Mainz November 1962	Reinhardt	LP: EMI 1C 063 30145
Munich December 1962	Bavarian RO Koetsier	LP: Philips 6520 022 CD: Philips 420 8522

Himmelsboten (Der Mondschein, er ist schon verblichen)

Munich Date uncertain	L.Kusche	Unpublished video recording

Die Händler und die Macher/Krämerspiegel

Munich Date uncertain	L.Kusche	Unpublished video recording

Ich trage meine Minne

Munich December 1962	Bavarian RO Koetsier	LP: Philips 6520 011 CD: Philips 420 8522
Munich June 1963	Giesen	Unpublished video recording
Edinburgh September 1966	Giesen	Unpublished radio broadcast

Morgen (Und morgen wird die Sonne wieder scheinen)

Munich December 1962	Bavarian RO Koetsier	LP: Philips 6520 022 CD: Philips 420 8522

Der Rosenkavalier

Buenos Aires October 1961	Role of Sänger Crespin, Meyer, Rothenberger, Böhme, H.Friedrich Teatro Colon Orchestra & Chorus Wallberg	Unpublished radio broadcast
Munich May 1965	Watson, Töpper, Köth, Böhme, Wiener Bavarian State Orchestra & Chorus Keilberth	Unpublished radio broadcast Gala performance for Queen Elizabeth II
Munich July 1966	Bjoner, Töpper, Köth, Böhme, Kusche Bavarian State Orchestra & Chorus Kempe	Unpublished radio broadcast

Der Rosenkavalier, Excerpt (Di rigori armato)

Vienna May 1966	Edelmann, Pantscheff VPO Cluytens	Unpublished radio broadcast

Salome

Vienna November 1965	Role of Narraboth Silja, Varnay, Stolze, Wächter VPO Kosler	Unpublished radio broadcast

Die schweigsame Frau

Salzburg August 1959	Role of Henry Güden, Milinkovic, Prey, Hotter Vienna Opera Chorus VPO Böhm	LP: Opera Discs OD 1000-1002 LP: Melodram MEL 105 CD: Melodram MEL 27071 CD: DG 445 3352/445 4912 Excerpt CD: Verona 28044-28045
Buenos Aires September 1961	Hallstein, Horakova, H.Friedrich, Böhme Teatro Colon Orchestra & Chorus Wallberg	Unpublished radio broadcast
Munich August 1962	Hallstein, Barth, Grumbach, Böhme Bavarian State Orchestra & Chorus Wallberg	Unpublished radio broadcast

Die schweigsame Frau, Unspecified extracts

Munich November 1960	Hallstein, Benningsen, Prey, Hotter Bavarian Radio Orchestra & Chorus Wallberg	Unpublished radio broadcast

Ständchen (Mach auf, mach auf, doch leise mein Kind!)

Munich December 1962	Bavarian RO Koetsier	LP: Philips 6520 022 CD: Philips 420 8522
Edinburgh September 1966	Giesen	Unpublished radio broadcast

Wie sollten wir geheim sie halten

Mainz November 1962	Reinhardt	LP: EMI 1C 063 30145

Zueignung (Ja, du weisst es, teure Seele!)

Mainz November 1962	Reinhardt	LP: EMI 1C 063 30145
Munich December 1962	Bavarian RO Koetsier	LP: Philips 6520 022 CD: Philips 420 8522

IGOR STRAVINSKY (1882-1971)

Oedipus rex

Stuttgart October 1959	<u>Role of Oedipus</u> Höffgen, Rohr, Cordes SDR Orchestra and Chorus Müller-Kray	Unpublished radio broadcast

Perséphone

Frankfurt November 1960	Schade Hessischer Rundfunk Orchestra & Chorus Dixon <u>Performed in German</u>	Unpublished radio broadcast

RICHARD TAUBER (1892-1948)

Der singende Traum, Excerpt (Du bist die Welt für mich)

Stuttgart November 1963	Südwestfunk- Unterhaltungs- Orchester Mattes	Unpublished radio broadcast
Munich May-June 1965	Lamy Choir Graunke SO Carste	LP: Karussell 535 009 LP: Heliodor (USA) H 25063/HS 25063 LP: Polydor Special 109 616-109 618

PIOTR TCHAIKOVSKY (1840-1893)

Evgeny Onegin

Munich October 1962	Role of Lensky Bremert, Töpper, Fassbaender, Prey, Yahia Bavarian State Orchestra & Chorus Keilberth Sung in German	CD: Gala GL 100.520 Also unpublished video recording

Evgeny Onegin, Querschnitt

Munich December 1962	Muszely, Prey, Frick Bavarian State Orchestra Zallinger Sung in German	LP: Electrola E 80743/STE 80743 LP: HMV ALP 2016/ASD 566 LP: EMI 1C 063 29011 LP: Angel 36376 Excerpts LP: Electrola E 80847/STE 80847 LP: EMI 1C 063 28173/1C187 29298-29299/ HQS 1168/EX 29 09883 LP: Angel 6157 CD: EMI CDC 747 6852/CZS 762 9932 CD: Nimbus NI 7851
Munich July 1966	Lear, Fassbaender, Fischer-Dieskau, Talvela Bavarian State Orchestra & Chorus Gerdes Sung in German	LP: DG LPEM 19 430/SLPEM 136 430/ 2535 323/2537 005 CD: DG 447 8182 Excerpts LP: DG 2721 230/413 8371 CD: DG 431 1102/435 1452 447 8182 contains an ensemble which was omitted from the LP Querschnitt

Evgeny Onegin, Excerpt (Faint echo of my youth)

Berlin January 1962	Berlin SO Stein Sung in German	Unpublished radio broadcast
Munich December 1963	Munich PO Stein Sung in German	Unpublished radio broadcast

Pique Dame, Querschnitt

Munich December 1962	Role of Hermann Muszely, Prey Bavarian State Orchestra Zallinger Sung in German	LP: Electrola E 80743/STE 80743 LP: HMV ALP 2016/ASD 566 LP: EMI 1C 063 29011 LP: Angel 36376 Excerpt LP: Electrola E 80847/STE 80847 LP: EMI 1C 063 28173/1C187 29298-29299/ HQS 1253/EX 29 09883 LP: Angel 6157 CD: EMI CZS 762 9932

None but the lonely heart

Berlin 1957	Berlin SO Becker Sung in German	LP: Eurodisc OE 88952/300 356.435/ 96 513/301 188.370 CD: Eurodisc GD 69018 CD: Munich Records MR 30007

GEORG PHILIPP TELEMANN (1681-1767)

Warum verstellst du die Gebärden?

Untertürkheim January 1958	Instrumentalists	Unpublished radio broadcast

270   Wunderlich

AMBROISE THOMAS (1811-1896)

Mignon, Querschnitt

Berlin June 1961	<u>Role of W.Meister</u> Lorengar, Pütz, Frick Komische Oper Chorus Berlin SO Klobucar <u>Sung in German</u>	LP: Electrola E 80639/STE 80639 LP: EMI EX 29 10251 CD: EMI CDZ 252 3832 <u>Excerpts</u> LP: Electrola E 80847/STE 80847 LP: EMI 1C 063 28173/1C187 29298-29299/ EX 29 09883 LP: Angel 6157 CD: EMI CZS 762 9932

HANS TOIFL (1900-1989)

Denk' dir, die Welt wär' ein Blumenstrauss

Munich August 1966	Spilar-Schrammeln	LP: Karussell 2415 030 LP: Heliodor (USA) H 25051/HS 25051 LP: Polydor Special 109 616-109 618

ENRICO TOSELLI (1883-1926)

Serenata

Munich May-June 1965	Lamy Choir Graunke SO Carste <u>Sung in German</u>	LP: Karussell 237 448/2562 040 LP: Heliodor (USA) H 25063/HS 25063 LP: Polydor Special 109 616-109 618

WALTER TRIEBL

Pfälzer Wein, Excerpts (1. Es gibt eine Frau; 2. Ja, der Pfälzer Wein!; 3. Man wird bescheiden)

Kaiserslautern March 1957	Sailer, Cordes Südwestfunk Orchestra & Chorus Smola	LP: Acanta BB 23245 (1) LP: Acanta 43.567 (2) Unpublished radio broadcast (3)

GIUSEPPE VERDI (1813-1901)

Don Carlo, Excerpt (Io l'ho perduta!)

Stuttgart January 1959	SDR Orchestra Müller-Kray Sung in German	LP: Acanta 23.568

Don Carlo, Excerpt (E lui! Desso, l'infante!)

Stuttgart January 1959	Wolansky SDR Orchestra Müller-Kray Sung in German	LP: Acanta 23.568
Munich January 1963	Prey Munich RO Stein Sung in German	LP: DG 2535 801/2721 230/413 8371 CD: DG 431 1102/435 1452

Rigoletto, Excerpt (Questa o'quella!)

Berlin 1958	Berlin SO Kraus Sung in German	LP: Europäischer Fonoklub 4233 LP: Eurodisc KR 70259/XA 25289/XA 85844/ XB 25968/XF 85175/96 513/300 356.435/ 301 185.370
Berlin July 1960	Berlin SO Klobucar Sung in German	LP: Electrola E 80847/STE 80847 LP: EMI 1C 063 28173/1C187 29298-29299 CD: EMI CZS 762 9932

Rigoletto, Excerpt (E il sol dell' anima)

Munich December 1961	Köth Munich RO Eichhorn Sung in German	LP: DG 2535 801/2721 230/413 8371 CD: DG 431 1102/435 1452
Munich September 1962	Köth Munich RO Eichhorn Sung in German	Unpublished radio broadcast

Rigoletto, Excerpt (La donna è mobile)

Berlin
1958
	Berlin SO
	Kraus
	Sung in German
		LP: Europäischer Fonoklub 4233
		LP: Eurodisc KR 70259/OU 27037/XA 25289/
		    XB 86838/XF 79915/300 356.435/96 513/
		    301 185.370

Berlin July 1960	Berlin SO Klobucar Sung in German	LP: Electrola E 80847/STE 80847 LP: EMI 1C 063 28173/SHZE 193/ 1C 187 29298-29299 LP: Angel 60043 CD: EMI CZS 762 9932
Baden-Baden November 1965	Südwestfunk Orchestra Smola	Unpublished radio broadcast

La Traviata

Munich March 1965	Role of Alfredo Stratas, Lenz, Prey Bavarian State Orchestra & Chorus Patané	LP: HRE Records HRE 334 LP: Di Stefano GDS 106 CD: Myto MCD 91648 CD: Orfeo C344 932I Excerpts CD: Verona 28044-28045 HRE names conductor as Votto; Verona names soprano as Güden

La Traviata, Querschnitt

Munich September 1966	Güden, Hellmann, Fischer-Dieskau Bavarian Radio Orchestra & Chorus Bartoletti Sung in German	LP: DG LPEM 19 431/SLPEM 136 431/2535 322 CD: DG 423 8732 Excerpts LP: DG 2535 627/2535 655/2562 040/ 2563 649/2721 230/413 8371 CD: DG 431 1102

La Traviata, Excerpt (E strano!/Sempre libera!)

Berlin 1960	Köth Berlin SO Klobucar <u>Sung in German</u>	LP: Eurodisc KR 70777

La Traviata, Excerpt (De' miei bollenti spiriti)

Berlin June 1961	Berlin SO Klobucar <u>Sung in German</u>	LP: Electrola E 80769/STE 80769 LP: EMI 1C 063 28420/1C187 29298-29299/ EX 29 09883 LP: Angel 6157 CD: EMI CDC 747 6852
Munich April 1965	Munich RO Eichhorn	Unpublished radio broadcast

La Traviata, Excerpt (Parigi o cara)

Munich December 1959	Köth Munich RO Zallinger <u>Sung in German</u>	Unpublished radio broadcast
Munich December 1963	Melander Munich RO Stein	Unpublished radio broadcast

Requiem

Stuttgart November 1960	Stader, Höffgen, Frick SDR Orchestra and Chorus Müller-Kray	CD: Myto MCD 91648 <u>Excerpts</u> CD: Verona 28044-28045

RICHARD WAGNER (1813-1883)

Der fliegende Holländer

Berlin
February 1960
	Role of Steuermann
	Schech, Wagner,
	Schock, Frick,
	Fischer-Dieskau
	Staatskapelle
	and Chorus
	Konwitschny
		LP: Electrola E 91056-91058/
		    STE 91056-91058
		LP: HMV ALP 1806-1808/ASD 385-387
		LP: EMI 1C 157 00104-00106/
		    1C183 30206-30208/1C149 30206-30208
		LP: Angel 3616
		CD: Berlin Classics BC 20972
		Excerpts
		LP: Electrola E 80847/STE 80847/
		    E 80677/STE 80677
		LP: EMI 1C 063 28173/HQS 1253/SHZE 154/
		    1C 187 29298-29299/EX 29 09883
		LP: Angel 6157
		CD: EMI CDZ 252 3812/CZS 767 1872

Tannhäuser

Berlin
October 1960
	Role of Walther
	von der Vogelweide
	Grümmer, Schech,
	Hopf, Frick,
	Fischer-Dieskau
	Staatskapelle
	and Chorus
	Konwitschny
		LP: Electrola E 91087-91090/
		    STE 91087-91090
		LP: HMV ALP 1876-1879/ASD 445-448
		LP: EMI 1C 153 30683-30686/
		    HQM 1081-1084/HQS 1081-1084
		LP: Angel 3620
		CD: EMI CMS 763 2142
		Excerpts
		LP: Electrola E 80638/STE 80638
		LP: HMV ALP 2005/ASD 555

GERHARD WINKLER

Das ist der Liebe Freud' und Leid; Sonne Italiens (both from the film Stimme der Sehnsucht)

Berlin 1957	FFB Orchestra Becker	LP: Eurodisc 300.356.435/96 513/ 301.188.370

HUGO WOLF (1860-1903)

Fussreise/Mörike-Lieder (Am frischgeschnitt'nen Wanderstab)

Mainz   Reinhardt   LP: EMI 1C 063 30145
November 1962

Italienisches Liederbuch: Gesegnet sei, durch den die Welt entstund; Nun lass uns Frieden schliessen; Hoffärtig seid Ihr; Wie soll ich fröhlich sein?; Nicht länger kann ich singen; O wüsstest du, wieviel ich deinetwegen

Mainz   Müller-Mayen   Unpublished radio broadcast
November 1955

Lied des transferierten Zettels (Die Schwalbe, die den Sommer bringt)

Munich   L.Kusche   Unpublished video recording
Date uncertain

Der Musikant (Wandern lieb' ich für mein Leben)

Mainz   Reinhardt   LP: EMI 1C 063 30145
November 1962

Nimmersatte Liebe (So ist die Lieb'!)

Mainz   Reinhardt   LP: EMI 1C 063 30145
November 1962

FRITZ WUNDERLICH (1930-1966)

Pfälzer Heimat (Ein Städtchen liegt im Pfälzerland)

Munich   Lamy Choir   45: Karussell 54 076
June 1965   Graunke SO
                Carste

FRIEDRICH ZEHM (born 1923)

7 Gesänge nach Gedichten von Georg Trakl

Freiburg 1955	Zehm	Unpublished radio broadcast

CARL ZELLER (1842-1898)

Der Obersteiger, Excerpt (Sei nicht bös')

Stuttgart 1957	Stuttgart PO Mareczek	LP: Vox STGBY 632 CD: ZYX Music CLS 42012

Der Vogelhändler

Cologne October 1960	Role of Adam Fahberg, Cramer, Lenz WDR Orchestra and Chorus Marszalek	Unpublished radio broadcast and soundtrack for TV recording Excerpts LP: RCA VL 30318 CD: Sonia 74505

Der Vogelhändler, Excerpts (Grüss euch Gott, alle miteinander!; Wie mein Ahnerl zwanzig Jahr')

Munich October 1957	Lamy Choir Munich RO Schmidt-Boelcke	LP: Europäischer Fonoklub 3204 LP: Eurodisc IE 70347/OE 88946/XF 76499/ OU 27037/XA 85844/300 356.435/96 513/ 301 188.370 CD: Eurodisc GD 69018 CD: Munich Records MR 30007

EMMERICH ZILLNER

Es steht ein alter Nussbaum drauss' in Heiligenstadt

Munich	Spilar-Schrammeln	LP: Karussell 535 009/2415 030
August 1966		LP: Heliodor (USA) H 25051/HS 25051
		LP: Polydor Special 109 616-109 618

CHRISTMAS CAROLS

Es ist ein Ros' entsprungen

Munich	Instrumentalists	LP: Polydor 249 090
June 1966	Neumeyer	LP: DG 2545 051
		CD: DG 419 5702

Es kommt ein Schiff geladen

Munich	Prey	LP: Polydor 249 090
June 1966	Instrumentalists	
	Neumeyer	

In dulci jubilo

Munich	Prey	LP: Polydor 249 090
June 1966	Instrumentalists	LP: DG 2721 213
	Neumeyer	CD: DG 423 4502

Maria durch ein' Dornwald ging

Munich	Prey	LP: Polydor 249 090
June 1966	Instrumentalists	LP: DG 2721 213
	Neumeyer	CD: DG 423 4502

Christmas carols/concluded

O Freude über Freude

Munich	Prey	LP: Polydor 249 090
June 1966	Instrumentalists	LP: DG 2721 213
	Neumeyer	CD: DG 423 4502

Stille Nacht, heilige Nacht

Munich	Chorus	LP: Europäischer Fonoklub 63913
1957	Stadlmair	LP: Eurodisc XR 79565
Munich	Prey	LP: Polydor 249 090
June 1966	Instrumentalists	
	Neumeyer	

Still, still, still, wer Gott erkennen will

Munich	Prey	LP: Polydor 249 090
June 1966	Instrumentalists	
	Neumeyer	

Vom Himmel hoch, o Englein kommt!

Munich	Prey	LP: Polydor 249 090
June 1966	Instrumentalists	LP: DG 2545 051
	Neumeyer	CD: DG 419 5702

Was soll das bedeuten, es taget ja schon

Munich	Prey	LP: Polydor 249 090
June 1966	Instrumentalists	LP: DG 2721 213
	Neumeyer	CD: DG 423 4502

ANONYMOUS AND FOLKSONGS

Aennchen von Tharau

Munich May-June 1965	Graunke SO Carste	LP: Karussell 237 448/2498 044 LP: Heliodor (USA) H 25063/HS 25063 LP: Polydor Special 109 616-109 618

Auf der Strasse von Dijon

Freiburg October 1954	Freiburg Mens' Choir Scherer	Unpublished radio broadcast

Du, du liegst mir im Herzen

Freiburg October 1954	Freiburg Mens' Choir Scherer	Unpublished radio broadcast

Ein Blümlein fein

Mainz Date uncertain	Instrumentalists	Unpublished radio broadcast

Ich schell' mein Horn

Mainz Date uncertain	Instrumentalists	Unpublished radio broadcast

Tiritomba (Sera giette, sera giette a la marina)

Munich January 1965	Lamy Choir Graunke SO Carste	LP: Karussell 2430 254 /2562 040 LP: Polydor Special 109 616-109 618 LP: DG 2721 230/413 8371
Kaiserslautern November 1965	Südwestfunk- Unterhaltungs- Orchester Smola	Unpublished radio broadcast

Discographies

The Furtwängler Sound, 5th edition
Composer and chronological discographies,
300 pages
Price £22 (£28 outside UK)

Teachers and pupils
Schwarzkopf / Ivogün / Cebotari /
Seinemeyer / Welitsch / Streich / Berger
7 separate discographies, 400 pages
Price £22 (£28 outside UK)

The post-war German tradition
Kempe / Keilberth / Sawallisch /Kubelik /
Cluytens
5 separate discographies, 300 pages
Price £22 (£28 outside UK)

**Mid-century conductors
and More Viennese singers**
Böhm / De Sabata / Knappertsbusch / Serafin /
Krauss / Dermota / Rysanek / Wächter /
Reining / Kunz
10 separate discographies, 420 pages
Price £18 (£22 outside UK)

Leopold Stokowski
Discography and concert register, 300 pages
Price £22 (£28 outside UK)

Makers of the Philharmonia
Galliera / Susskind / Kletzki / Malko / Matacic /
Dobrowen / Kurtz / Fistoulari
8 separate discographies, 300 pages
Price £22 (£28 outside UK)

A notable quartet
Janowitz / Ludwig / Gedda / Fischer-Dieskau
4 separate discographies, 600 pages
Price £20 (£25 outside UK)

Musical knights
Wood / Beecham / Boult / Barbirolli /Goodall /
Sargent
6 separate discographies, 400 pages
Price £20 (£25 outside UK)

Prices include postage
order from: John Hunt, Flat 6,
37 Chester Way, London SE11 4UR

CREDITS

Valuable help in the preparation of these
discographies came from:

Richard Chlupaty, London
Dennis Davis, London
Clifford Elkin, Glasgow
Mathias Erhard, Berlin
Edward Johnson, London
Alan Newcombe, Hamburg
Alan Sanders, Richmond
Malcolm Walker, Harrow

Discographies by Travis & Emery:
Discographies by John Hunt.

1987: 978-1-906857-14-1: From Adam to Webern: the Recordings of von Karajan.
1991: 978-0-951026-83-0: 3 Italian Conductors and 7 Viennese Sopranos: 10 Discographies: Arturo Toscanini, Guido Cantelli, Carlo Maria Giulini, Elisabeth Schwarzkopf, Irmgard Seefried, Elisabeth Gruemmer, Sena Jurinac, Hilde Gueden, Lisa Della Casa, Rita Streich.
1992: 978-0-951026-85-4: Mid-Century Conductors and More Viennese Singers: 10 Discographies: Karl Boehm, Victor De Sabata, Hans Knappertsbusch, Tullio Serafin, Clemens Krauss, Anton Dermota, Leonie Rysanek, Eberhard Waechter, Maria Reining, Erich Kunz.
1993: 978-0-951026-87-8: More 20th Century Conductors: 7 Discographies: Eugen Jochum, Ferenc Fricsay, Carl Schuricht, Felix Weingartner, Josef Krips, Otto Klemperer, Erich Kleiber.
1994: 978-0-951026-88-5: Giants of the Keyboard: 6 Discographies: Wilhelm Kempff, Walter Gieseking, Edwin Fischer, Clara Haskil, Wilhelm Backhaus, Artur Schnabel.
1994: 978-0-951026-89-2: Six Wagnerian Sopranos: 6 Discographies: Frieda Leider, Kirsten Flagstad, Astrid Varnay, Martha Moedl, Birgit Nilsson, Gwyneth Jones.
1995: 978-0-952582-70-0: Musical Knights: 6 Discographies: Henry Wood, Thomas Beecham, Adrian Boult, John Barbirolli, Reginald Goodall, Malcolm Sargent.
1995: 978-0-952582-71-7: A Notable Quartet: 4 Discographies: Gundula Janowitz, Christa Ludwig, Nicolai Gedda, Dietrich Fischer-Dieskau.
1996: 978-0-952582-72-4: The Post-War German Tradition: 5 Discographies: Rudolf Kempe, Joseph Keilberth, Wolfgang Sawallisch, Rafael Kubelik, Andre Cluytens.
1996: 978-0-952582-73-1: Teachers and Pupils: 7 Discographies: Elisabeth Schwarzkopf, Maria Ivoguen, Maria Cebotari, Meta Seinemeyer, Ljuba Welitsch, Rita Streich, Erna Berger.
1996: 978-0-952582-77-9: Tenors in a Lyric Tradition: 3 Discographies: Peter Anders, Walther Ludwig, Fritz Wunderlich.
1997: 978-0-952582-78-6: The Lyric Baritone: 5 Discographies: Hans Reinmar, Gerhard Huesch, Josef Metternich, Hermann Uhde, Eberhard Waechter.
1997: 978-0-952582-79-3: Hungarians in Exile: 3 Discographies: Fritz Reiner, Antal Dorati, George Szell.
1997: 978-1-901395-00-6: The Art of the Diva: 3 Discographies: Claudia Muzio, Maria Callas, Magda Olivero.
1997: 978-1-901395-01-3: Metropolitan Sopranos: 4 Discographies: Rosa Ponselle, Eleanor Steber, Zinka Milanov, Leontyne Price.
1997: 978-1-901395-02-0: Back From The Shadows: 4 Discographies: Willem Mengelberg, Dimitri Mitropoulos, Hermann Abendroth, Eduard Van Beinum.
1997: 978-1-901395-03-7: More Musical Knights: 4 Discographies: Hamilton Harty, Charles Mackerras, Simon Rattle, John Pritchard.
1998: 978-1-901395-94-5: Conductors On The Yellow Label: 8 Discographies: Fritz Lehmann, Ferdinand Leitner, Ferenc Fricsay, Eugen Jochum, Leopold Ludwig, Artur Rother, Franz Konwitschny, Igor Markevitch.
1998: 978-1-901395-95-2: More Giants of the Keyboard: 5 Discographies: Claudio Arrau, Gyorgy Cziffra, Vladimir Horowitz, Dinu Lipatti, Artur Rubinstein.
1998: 978-1-901395-96-9: Mezzo and Contraltos: 5 Discographies: Janet Baker, Margarete Klose, Kathleen Ferrier, Giulietta Simionato, Elisabeth Hoengen.

1999: 978-1-901395-97-6: The Furtwaengler Sound Sixth Edition: Discography and Concert Listing.
1999: 978-1-901395-98-3: The Great Dictators: 3 Discographies: Evgeny Mravinsky, Artur Rodzinski, Sergiu Celibidache.
1999: 978-1-901395-99-0: Sviatoslav Richter: Pianist of the Century: Discography.
2000: 978-1-901395-04-4: Philharmonic Autocrat 1: Discography of: Herbert Von Karajan [Third Edition].
2000: 978-1-901395-05-1: Wiener Philharmoniker 1 - Vienna Philharmonic and Vienna State Opera Orchestras: Discography Part 1 1905-1954.
2000: 978-1-901395-06-8: Wiener Philharmoniker 2 - Vienna Philharmonic and Vienna State Opera Orchestras: Discography Part 2 1954-1989.
2001: 978-1-901395-07-5: Gramophone Stalwarts: 3 Separate Discographies: Bruno Walter, Erich Leinsdorf, Georg Solti.
2001: 978-1-901395-08-2: Singers of the Third Reich: 5 Discographies: Helge Roswaenge, Tiana Lemnitz, Franz Voelker, Maria Mueller, Max Lorenz.
2001: 978-1-901395-09-9: Philharmonic Autocrat 2: Concert Register of Herbert Von Karajan Second Edition.
2002: 978-1-901395-10-5: Sächsische Staatskapelle Dresden: Complete Discography.
2002: 978-1-901395-11-2: Carlo Maria Giulini: Discography and Concert Register.
2002: 978-1-901395-12-9: Pianists For The Connoisseur: 6 Discographies: Arturo Benedetti Michelangeli, Alfred Cortot, Alexis Weissenberg, Clifford Curzon, Solomon, Elly Ney.
2003: 978-1-901395-14-3: Singers on the Yellow Label: 7 Discographies: Maria Stader, Elfriede Troetschel, Annelies Kupper, Wolfgang Windgassen, Ernst Haefliger, Josef Greindl, Kim Borg.
2003: 978-1-901395-15-0: A Gallic Trio: 3 Discographies: Charles Muench, Paul Paray, Pierre Monteux.
2004: 978-1-901395-16-7: Antal Dorati 1906-1988: Discography and Concert Register.
2004: 978-1-901395-17-4: Columbia 33CX Label Discography.
2004: 978-1-901395-18-1: Great Violinists: 3 Discographies: David Oistrakh, Wolfgang Schneiderhan, Arthur Grumiaux.
2006: 978-1-901395-19-8: Leopold Stokowski: Second Edition of the Discography.
2006: 978-1-901395-20-4: Wagner Im Festspielhaus: Discography of the Bayreuth Festival.
2006: 978-1-901395-21-1: Her Master's Voice: Concert Register and Discography of Dame Elisabeth Schwarzkopf [Third Edition].
2007: 978-1-901395-22-8: Hans Knappertsbusch: Kna: Concert Register and Discography of Hans Knappertsbusch, 1888-1965. Second Edition.
2008: 978-1-901395-23-5: Philips Minigroove: Second Extended Version of the European Discography.
2009: 978-1-901395--24-2: American Classics: The Discographies of Leonard Bernstein and Eugene Ormandy.

Discography by Stephen J. Pettitt, edited by John Hunt:
1987: 978-1-906857-16-5: Philharmonia Orchestra: Complete Discography 1945-1987

Available from: Travis & Emery at 17 Cecil Court, London, UK. (+44) 20 7 240 2129. email on sales@travis-and-emery.com .

© Travis & Emery 2009

Music and Books published by Travis & Emery Music Bookshop:

Anon.: Hymnarium Sarisburiense, cum Rubricis et Notis Musicis.
Agricola, Johann Friedrich from Tosi: Anleitung zur Singkunst.
Bach, C.P.E.: edited W. Emery: Nekrolog or Obituary Notice of J.S. Bach.
Bateson, Naomi Judith: Alcock of Salisbury
Bathe, William: A Briefe Introduction to the Skill of Song
Bax, Arnold: Symphony #5, Arranged for Piano Four Hands by Walter Emery
Burney, Charles: The Present State of Music in France and Italy
Burney, Charles: The Present State of Music in Germany, The Netherlands ...
Burney, Charles: An Account of the Musical Performances ... Handel
Burney, Karl: Nachricht von Georg Friedrich Handel's Lebensumstanden.
Cobbett, W.W.: Cobbett's Cyclopedic Survey of Chamber Music. (2 vols.)
Corrette, Michel: Le Maitre de Clavecin
Crimp, Bryan: Dear Mr. Rosenthal ... Dear Mr. Gaisberg ...
Crimp, Bryan: Solo: The Biography of Solomon
d'Indy, Vincent: Beethoven: Biographie Critique
d'Indy, Vincent: Beethoven: A Critical Biography
d'Indy, Vincent: César Franck (in French)
Frescobaldi, Girolamo: D'Arie Musicali per Cantarsi. Primo & Secondo Libro.
Geminiani, Francesco: The Art of Playing the Violin.
Handel; Purcell; Boyce; Geene et al: Calliope or English Harmony: Volume First.
Hawkins, John: A General History of the Science and Practice of Music (5 vols.)
Herbert-Caesari, Edgar: The Science and Sensations of Vocal Tone
Herbert-Caesari, Edgar: Vocal Truth
Hopkins and Rimboult: The Organ. Its History and Construction.
Hunt, John: Adam to Webern: the recordings of von Karajan
Isaacs, Lewis: Hänsel and Gretel. A Guide to Humperdinck's Opera.
Isaacs, Lewis: Königskinder (Royal Children) A Guide to Humperdinck's Opera.
Lacassagne, M. l'Abbé Joseph : Traité Général des élémens du Chant.
Lascelles (née Catley), Anne: The Life of Miss Anne Catley.
Mainwaring, John: Memoirs of the Life of the Late George Frederic Handel
Malcolm, Alexander: A Treaty of Music: Speculative, Practical and Historical
Marx, Adolph Bernhard: Die Kunst des Gesanges, Theoretisch-Practisch
May, Florence: The Life of Brahms
Mellers, Wilfrid: Angels of the Night: Popular Female Singers of Our Time
Mellers, Wilfrid: Bach and the Dance of God
Mellers, Wilfrid: Beethoven and the Voice of God

Travis & Emery Music Bookshop
17 Cecil Court, London, WC2N 4EZ, United Kingdom.
Tel. (+44) 20 7240 2129

Music and Books published by Travis & Emery Music Bookshop:
Mellers, Wilfrid: Caliban Reborn - Renewal in Twentieth Century Music
Mellers, Wilfrid: François Couperin and the French Classical Tradition
Mellers, Wilfrid: Harmonious Meeting
Mellers, Wilfrid: Le Jardin Retrouvé, The Music of Frederic Mompou
Mellers, Wilfrid: Music and Society, England and the European Tradition
Mellers, Wilfrid: Music in a New Found Land: ... ... American Music
Mellers, Wilfrid: Romanticism and the Twentieth Century (from 1800)
Mellers, Wilfrid: The Masks of Orpheus: ...... the Story of European Music.
Mellers, Wilfrid: The Sonata Principle (from c. 1750)
Mellers, Wilfrid: Vaughan Williams and the Vision of Albion
Panchianio, Cattuffio: Rutzvanscad Il Giovine
Pearce, Charles: Sims Reeves, Fifty Years of Music in England.
Playford, John: An Introduction to the Skill of Musick.
Purcell, Henry et al: Harmonia Sacra ... The First Book, (1726)
Purcell, Henry et al: Harmonia Sacra ... Book II (1726)
Quantz, Johann: Versuch einer Anweisung die Flöte traversiere zu spielen.
Rameau, Jean-Philippe: Code de Musique Pratique, ou Methodes.
Rastall, Richard: The Notation of Western Music.
Rimbault, Edward: The Pianoforte, Its Origins, Progress, and Construction.
Rousseau, Jean Jacques: Dictionnaire de Musique
Rubinstein, Anton : Guide to the proper use of the Pianoforte Pedals.
Sainsbury, John S.: Dictionary of Musicians. Vol. 1. (1825). 2 vols.
Simpson, Christopher: A Compendium of Practical Musick in Five Parts
Spohr, Louis: Autobiography
Spohr, Louis: Grand Violin School
Tans'ur, William: A New Musical Grammar; or The Harmonical Spectator
Terry, Charles Sanford: Four-Part Chorals of J.S. Bach. (German & English)
Terry, Charles Sanford: Joh. Seb. Bach, Cantata Texts, Sacred and Secular.
Terry, Charles Sanford: The Origins of the Family of Bach Musicians.
Tosi, Pierfrancesco: Opinioni de' Cantori Antichi, e Moderni
Van der Straeten, Edmund: History of the Violoncello, The Viol da Gamba ...
Van der Straeten, Edmund: History of the Violin, Its Ancestors... (2 vols.)
Walther, J. G.: Musicalisches Lexikon ober Musicalische Bibliothec

Travis & Emery Music Bookshop
17 Cecil Court, London, WC2N 4EZ, United Kingdom.
Tel. (+44) 20 7240 2129

© Travis & Emery 2009

www.ingramcontent.com/pod-product-compliance
Lightning Source LLC
Chambersburg PA
CBHW070938230426
43666CB00011B/2485